Freedom From Codependency

A Christian Response

Philip St. Romain

LIGUORI
PUBLICATIONS

One Liguori Drive
Liguori, Missouri 63057-9999
(314) 464-2500

Imprimi Potest:
James Shea, C.SS.R.
Provincial, St. Louis Province
The Redemptorists

Imprimatur:
Monsignor Maurice F. Byrne
Vice Chancellor, Archdiocese of St. Louis

ISBN 0-89243-336-1
Library of Congress Catalog Card Number: 90-64273

Cover design by Chris Sharp

Contents

Acknowledgments

Years ago, when I first attended an Al-Anon meeting, the chairperson introduced herself as a grateful codependent. She meant that her codependency taught her that she was powerless over other people and led her to the program of Al-Anon with its life-saving message. In a similar vein, I would like to express gratitude to the many addicts I have lived with and worked with through the years as both a family member, a roommate, and a counselor. I have learned more about the meaning of Christian love through my relationships with addicts than I have from anything else.

Special thanks go to Benny McCardle, who invited me to begin work in the field of substance abuse back in 1980 and who has been an invaluable dialogue partner in developing these thoughts on Christian and codependent loving.

Helpful feedback concerning different parts of this book was offered by several ministers, most notably Rev. John Edmunds, S.T., Rev. Daniel Drinan, C.M.F., Rev. Robert Marcell, Rev. Walter Smith, Tom Artz, and the editorial staff of Liguori Publications. Substance-abuse counselors providing feedback were Ellen Calvert, C.S.A.C., Shirley Smith, C.S.A.C., Barry Mangham, C.S.A.C., Deborah Duckworth, B.C.S.W., and Barbara Sinkiewicz, R.N., C.S.A.C.

The writings of Dr. Anne Wilson Schaef provided both inspiration and a structure for developing this book. In the summer of

1988, when I informed Dr. Schaef of this present work, she responded immediately with words of encouragement and support.

My wife, Lisa Bellecci-St. Romain, has been most helpful through the years by working with me to detach from codependent ways of relating. Consequently, we are experiencing both belonging and freedom in our relationship. It's getting better and better all the time. Thanks, Lis!

Finally, I wish to acknowledge my children, Rita, Theresa, and Paul, for the growth I am experiencing because of them. Parenting can easily develop into a codependent role — as it has, indeed, for me at times. But we've all hung in there together, and parenting, too, has become for me an enjoyable experience.

Philip St. Romain

CHAPTER ONE
What Is Codependency?

During the past fifteen years, hundreds of thousands of individuals and their families have undergone therapy for chemical dependency. For these people, terms such as codependency, ACOA (Adult Children of Alcoholics), relapse, and recovery have become household words. The language of addiction and recovery is already shaping the way they are coming to grips with issues of identity, relationships, and spiritual growth.

For many ministers and laypeople in the Church, the concept of codependency is the most valuable contribution of the recovery movement to contemporary life. People who are not alcoholics, drug addicts, compulsive overeaters, or gamblers (the addictions most recognized by the public) often view the addiction/recovery model of mental and spiritual health as an irrelevancy unconnected to their own lives. "I'm glad there is help for those other people" expresses their attitude.

The concept of codependency, however, has immensely broadened our understanding of the nature and pervasiveness of addiction in our culture. The term *codependency* was first used to describe the dysfunctional patterns of thinking and behaving evidenced by spouses and children of chemically dependent people, but within the past ten years the concept has taken on a much wider application. We have come to see that spouses of alcoholics are not the only ones who allow people and circumstances outside their control to determine their experiences of happiness and pain. This is what codependents do, and it is a very painful predicament.

A Case Study

No one who drinks alcohol sets out to become an alcoholic. By the same token, no one enters a relationship with another human being intending to become a codependent.

This was certainly true for Jane. When she and Tom married, they were both healthy young people. They had college degrees, satisfying jobs, close relationships with friends and family members, enjoyable hobbies, and an interest in their church community. They also had each other, and their relationship as a couple was primary to them. They also enjoyed their jobs, friends, family, hobbies, and church, so they were able to keep a balance in their relationship. They did not smother each other with their love. After two years of marriage their first child was born and Tom and Jane appeared to be on their way to realizing the great American dream.

About that time Tom also got a significant promotion in his job. He accepted the position of supervisor over a large region of his company. This promotion brought a considerable pay raise that enabled him and Jane to purchase a new home for their growing family and allowed Jane to remain at home with Stacey, their baby girl. The unpleasant side of the promotion was that it called for Tom to travel out of town for several nights a month. Since their relationship was strong, however, Jane and Tom believed they could handle it.

During his travels away from home, Tom attended many business luncheons and dinners. Inevitably, alcohol was served before and during these meals. Considering himself a social drinker — he seldom drank to excess, even in college — he saw no reason to refuse a drink or two during these meetings. Besides, he told himself, with everyone else drinking, it would have been impolite to abstain. Since Tom seemed his usual self upon his return from each of these trips, there was no problem.

Tom did not know that his grandfather had been an alcoholic. His dad never drank and had never spoken of Grandpa's alcoholism. Grandpa had managed to stay sober during the years when Tom knew him, and the family never discussed his previous drinking years. Yet, like his grandfather, Tom had a biochemistry capable of developing alcoholism. In truth, he liked the way he felt when he drank, and he found himself drinking more and more at his business meals. He also saw no reason to avoid drinking at home, since he was an adult and could afford it. These two factors — enjoying the feeling alcohol gives and the ability to use more and more of the drug (tolerance) — are necessary if alcoholism is to develop. Like a biochemistry predisposed to alcoholism, these two factors are inherited.

At first Jane saw nothing wrong with Tom's drinking at home. Unlike Tom, she did know something about alcoholism. Her father was an alcoholic, and she had grown up witnessing firsthand his drunkenness and quarrels with her mother. Like Tom's grandfather, Jane's father had quit drinking, but not until Jane was a teenager. Frequently angry and cranky, he boasted about quitting on his own, telling his family they should be grateful that at least he wasn't drinking anymore. Jane knew what heavy drinking was like, and Tom was no heavy drinker — at least not at first.

After seven years of marriage, Tom's drinking had steadily increased, and he began to give up healthy involvements. He seldom went to church, visited with family members, or played golf. Tom and Jane now had three young children, and Tom frequently complained about the noise and normal clutter children create in a home. His life consisted of going off on business trips, working long hours when he was in town, drinking alcohol, and watching television. Except for sex, he showed little interest in Jane. After seven years of marriage, Tom had become a chronic alcoholic.

Because Tom's alcoholism developed slowly, Jane did not recognize it for what it was. She rationalized that the longer periods he spent away from home were part of his job. She explained his increased drinking as just his way of relaxing after long hours at work. It bothered her that he had little time for family, friends, hobbies, and church; but she figured that it was all a passing phase in their life together. One day, she reasoned, Tom's work would let up and they could go back to being the happy couple they once were. She was lonely, but her days were so filled with the needs of their three small children that she could avoid facing this loneliness.

When Tom finally started getting drunk at home, Jane knew he had a problem; but she didn't know what to do. Her dad had stopped on his own; maybe Tom would too. She asked him to stop many times, but each time this only started an argument that led to more drinking. There were even times when Tom blamed her for his drinking — telling her she had gotten fat and wasn't attractive anymore. It was true, she admitted, that she had put on a few pounds. And no, she didn't feel like having sex.

Realizing that Tom was pulling away from her and everything they had once held dear, Jane tried hard to make him happy and avoid making him mad. She cooked his favorite meals, kept the house clean, rented videotapes for the kids to watch so they would be quiet when he was home, and even submitted to more frequent sex with him. She also assumed responsibilities that had once been his — like paying the bills, mowing the lawn, and putting out the garbage. Eventually, her life became focused on keeping Tom happy so he wouldn't drink.

Her efforts didn't work, however. Although at times Tom did show appreciation for all Jane did for him, more often he found something to complain about. And he didn't stop drinking. In fact, his drinking increased. Jane became even more determined than ever to bring him back.

Then one day while shopping at the supermarket, Jane met her friend Paula, who asked how she was doing.

"Fine!" Jane responded. "Tom's really doing well at work, and the kids are making good grades at school."

Jane was unaware that Paula, who attended Al-Anon meetings, knew about Tom's drinking problem. Like many people in her situation, Jane deluded herself that she had succeeded in hiding their family "secret" from the rest of the world. Paula decided to ease into the topic by asking why Jane had dropped out of the bowling league they both had been part of for years.

"There's just too much going on at home," Jane responded. "Tom and the kids seem to need me more than ever."

"I haven't seen you at church lately, either," Paula noted.

Jane began to feel guilty, but she responded defensively. "Well, we just don't like that new pastor. All he ever talks about is money!"

"I think Father Jones is doing a good job," Paula replied. "Are you sure everything's okay with you? You seem distracted, preoccupied — not your old self at all."

By this time Jane couldn't wait to get out of the store. She considered moving to another line, but this would be difficult with Paula standing behind her. Besides, she was already running late, and Tom would surely be angry, since she left him at home with the kids. Preoccupied with these worries, she failed to notice that she hadn't answered Paula's question.

"What's wrong, Jane?" Paula finally asked. "Is it something with you and Tom? Bill and I have been through it too, but things are much better since he went through treatment for his drinking."

"Drinking!" Jane exclaimed, feeling insulted. "Tom doesn't have a drinking problem! I mean, he drinks a little every now and then, but he still has his job, and he's home every night he's in town!"

"I didn't say Tom had a drinking problem," Paula replied.

"Well, he doesn't!" Jane affirmed. "And I'm okay too — just a little tired, that's all. We're doing okay."

Paula nodded sadly, seeing in Jane the person she had been two years before.

Characteristics of Codependents

During my years of counseling with hundreds of codependents, I have often been struck by the consistency of the characteristics they presented. This consistency holds true for chemically dependent people as well; the people are unique, but their disease is not. It is the same with measles too, I suppose; the symptomatology is similar across a wide spectrum of people. This consistency of symptoms convinces me that codependency is an addictive disease process and not merely a "personality type."

The symptoms of codependency are the same as those for other addictions. The only difference is that while other addicts are focused on alcohol, drugs, work, gambling, sex, and so forth, codependents are focused on other people — usually one person in particular. The long-term characteristics of codependency are described below.

1. *External reference.* Codependents are focused on other people as the source of their happiness and/or pain.

2. *Controlling behavior.* Because other people are responsible for the codependent's happiness, codependents attempt to influence these others to act approvingly toward the codependent. Several strategies are employed:

- **a.** *People-pleasing.* Doing what the other likes or wants, even when the codependent does not feel like doing it or when it goes against his or her values.
- **b.** *Caretaking or enabling behavior.* Doing for others what they can and should do for themselves. Taking over the responsibilities of others and lying for others.
- **c.** *Approval-seeking.* Doing or saying what will impress others to gain their approval — even if it means exaggerating or being dishonest.
- **d.** *Nagging and criticizing.* If others cannot be influenced through people-pleasing, caretaking, and approval-seeking behavior, then the codependent attempts to influence them through shame and disapproval.

3. *Emotional pain.* Codependents are usually afraid of losing the persons upon whom they are focused. They also feel guilty about some of their people-pleasing and caretaking behaviors. They are hurt, angry, and resentful toward others because of the way these others treat them. They feel a sense of inadequacy and failure because they are frequently rejected. And finally, they feel very lonely.

4. *Rigid defense system.* Instead of openly expressing their inner pain, codependents distort this pain through defensive strategies that minimize the seriousness of their predicament. They deny and minimize their problems, attack those who question them about their feelings, blame others (such as the children) for their unhealthy relationship, rationalize and justify their situation, or simply remain silent about what's going on inside themselves. As a result of these defenses, codependents get no relief from their emotional pain and continue to accumulate fear, guilt, shame, and resentment. They are very miserable inside and frequently resort to addictions (food, alcohol, drugs, shopping, and so forth) to deal with this pain.

5. *Delusional beliefs.* Codependents believe that the relationship is "not all that bad" and "will get better." Even after being abused many times by another, they think, "This time he really means it!" They also believe that eventually they will be successful at controlling others if they can find the right combination of enabling, people-pleasing, and approval-seeking behaviors.

6. *Loss of self.* As a result of focusing on others, denying themselves, compromising their values, and holding their pain inside, codependents eventually lose touch with their own inner dynamism. This loss of self, in turn, moves them to focus more intently on getting other people to give them what they lack inside, mainly self-esteem and self-love. Because one person cannot give another self-esteem and self-love, the codependent's loss of self only intensifies.

7. *Martyr complex.* In an attempt to salvage a sense of self-worth, codependents sometimes view themselves as victims and martyrs. Lacking self-love, they use self-pity as a way to assuage their inner pain. When others say, "I don't know how you can live with him; you must be a saint," codependents feel validated as martyrs.

Obviously, these characteristics of codependents describe a person who is very, very miserable. Friends and acquaintances often ask, "Why do codependents allow themselves to deteriorate so badly? Why don't they get a grip, stand up for themselves, and take better care of themselves?"

These questions will be answered in the next section, Codependency as Addiction. For now, however, I will say that no person ever intends to become a codependent — just as no one intends to become an alcoholic or drug addict. Considering the example of Tom and Jane, we can easily see the insidious nature of addictions. Neither intended to become an addict. Codependency progressed slowly. The progressive loss of inner freedom makes one increasingly vulnerable to the addictive processes at work in the mind. In short, it's not the codependent's fault that this has happened.

Codependency as Addiction

The history of recovery groups in this country has much to teach us about codependency. Typically, spouses of alcoholics viewed the behavior of the alcoholic as the source of all their marital problems. For decades counselors and clergy have heard, "If he (she) stops drinking, I'll be okay." Then in the 1930s, Alcoholics Anonymous, which has helped millions of people recover from alcoholism, was founded. The alcoholic *did* stop drinking and *did* begin to experience a much more enjoyable life. Most curiously, however, the alcoholic's spouse often did not become okay as a result. Quite frequently the spouse remained resentful, external-referenced, and anxious about relapse. "What if it doesn't last?" became the new focus of anxiety.

In other words, the alcoholic's spouse did not become well simply because the alcoholic got better. These spouses discovered that living with addiction had changed them. They were not the people they had been before their lives began to deteriorate. Furthermore, they did not even know what was wrong or what to do to help themselves. They continued to nag and caretake though there was no longer a need to do so. In time, enough spouses and family members recognized that they needed precisely the kind of help for themselves that alcoholics were finding in AA. They began meeting with others in the same predicament to talk about how they had been affected, and they began using the Twelve Steps of AA to recover their lost selfhood. Al-Anon, the fellowship that grew out of these meetings, endures as one of the most positive influences for mental and spiritual health in the world today.

The situation leading to the formation of Al-Anon is one indication that codependency is an addictive disease process. Another indication is the way untreated codependents continue to make the same mistakes again and again. For example, I once counseled a man who had married seven women — all of them alcoholic. How do we explain such a behavior pattern? As a codependent not working a recovery program, he was compulsively driven to find someone else to focus upon in his life. Single alcoholic women need someone to take care of them, so his codependency and their alcoholism fit together like two pieces in a puzzle.

Nevertheless, many psychiatrists, social workers, and other counselors do not treat codependency as an addiction (although a growing number do). They see all the characteristics mentioned in the previous section and try to work on these issues. People in the early stages of the addiction may get all the help they need by learning to boost self-esteem and becoming assertive of their needs. Codependents in the later stages, however, will need more help than this. Tragically, many codependents continue meeting month after month and year after year with counselors, often without making significant progress.

The recognition of addiction as a whole system of consciousness focusing on a specific center — the addictive fix — is the most significant contribution to mental health from the addictive counseling field. Addiction is like a mind within the mind — a kind of hurricane turning in consciousness. Like a hurricane, the storm of addictive consciousness is organized around a center. For alcoholics this center is drinking; for gamblers it is gambling; for codependents it is controlling another person.

If the addictive system is to be disempowered, the first step is giving up the fix. The alcoholic must stop drinking; the gambler must stop gambling; the codependent must stop enabling, people-pleasing, nagging, and using other means to try to control people. This is not all there is to recovery, of course, but it is a beginning. If the fix is not given up, the addictive system will continue to function. Once the fix is given up, the stormy feelings and delusional beliefs persist, but they can be dealt with over time.

Another contribution of the addiction field is the recognition of fix-indulgence as a spiritual issue. Whatever our lives are centered on — that is our god. Therefore, recovery calls for finding a new center — a Higher Power — around which to rehabilitate the mind. It is almost impossible to recover from any addiction without finding a new center. And it is here that conventional forms of psychotherapy fail people most acutely. Because they deal only with the clouds in the storm and avoid the issues of centeredness and spirituality, conventional therapies usually provide, at best, band-aid solutions for codependents in distress.

Stages of Codependency

Most of our discussion up to this point has focused on codependency as it is manifested in its later stages. Like other addictions, however, codependency develops through a series of earlier stages.

People are not born codependents. Codependency is a learned pattern of dysfunctional thinking, deciding, and behaving that develops gradually over time. Using the addiction model as our guide, we can identify several turning points in the progression of codependency.

1. *Experimentation.* We learn that people-pleasing and approval-seeking behavior gives us influence in relationships. We also learn to meet some of our emotional needs in this manner.

2. *Early stage.* Our people-pleasing and approval-seeking behavior gets results. We get "high" on the praise and gratitude that others accord us when we please them or impress them. We make a commitment to using these behaviors in our relationships.

3. *Middle stage.* We begin giving up healthy involvements, usually because we find ourselves tied to an emotionally demanding person or situation. We try harder to please and impress, but results are sporadic. Consequently, we begin to experience hurt, disappointment, and resentment.

4. *Chronic stage.* With the accumulation of emotional pain, we become compulsively focused on the object of our pain — on trying to control it or transform it. Neuroses and even psychoses begin developing. Physical health suffers. Many consequences develop in relationships. Other addictions spin off.

5. *Terminal stage.* Consciousness is fixated on the object of our pain. Physical and mental health deteriorate rapidly.

Perhaps the literature on codependency has been so well received by the public because many people are in at least the early and middle stages of codependency. Who is there among us who has never been caught up in people-pleasing and approval-seeking behavior? All that is lacking for this behavior to proceed into chronic addiction is a dysfunctional environment of some kind. Many people who live with addicts or who find themselves tied to other emotionally demanding situations in the home, school, church, or workplace find themselves in exactly such an environment.

In addition to the addiction and psychiatric views of codependency, there is another approach commonly found among the churches. We shall call this the moralistic model. A counselor working from this approach sees addictions in terms of moral weakness or moral strength. Alcoholics, for example, are considered sinners. It is held that they could stop drinking if they wanted to and if they called upon God for help. According to this reasoning, alcoholics who do not stop drinking must not want to stop. Hence, they must not care for their families; therefore, they are selfish sinners — bad people!

Unfortunately, the moralistic approach to addictions is by no means a rare phenomenon. It is the approach taken by many Fundamentalist pastors, and it also influences the attitudes of many in the mainline Christian churches.

Counselors working out of the addiction model will certainly acknowledge that addicts violate their own ethical values. Unlike the moralistic counselors, however, addiction-model counselors maintain that the ethical deterioration of the addict is a *consequence* of addiction — not the cause. The importance of this distinction cannot be overstated. In the moralistic model, addicts are judged as bad people who need to become good; in the addiction model, addicts are viewed as sick people who need to recover. There is a difference between the labels "bad" and "sick," especially when applied to the addict struggling to recover.

Because moralistic counselors view alcoholics (sex addicts, gamblers, and so on) as bad people, they naturally see codependents as good people. They say things like "I don't know how she could live with him; she must be a saint!" In counseling the codependent, they frequently reinforce the codependent's view of herself or himself as a martyr suffering through this life for the sake of a "treasure in heaven." They frequently discourage the codependent from leaving the marriage, even if it is abusive, for such moralizers are opposed to separation and divorce. Their counseling strategy often focuses on helping the codependent find ways to change the addict (or other cause he or she is focused upon). In these and many other ways, moralistic counselors actually enable codependents to progress in their illness.

Expanding the Metaphor

Almost everything we have said so far about codependency has been in the context of living with chemical dependency. This is the context in which codependency was first described and recognized as an addictive disorder in its own right.

During the past ten years, however, the concept of codependency has been extended beyond the context of chemical dependency. Many who were not living with chemically dependent people nevertheless recognized in themselves the same addictive patterns described in this chapter. Living with gamblers, work addicts, religion addicts, sex addicts, and chronically ill and needy people often leads to codependency. In addition, some romantic relationships become addictive even when there is no addiction or physical illness involved.

Despite a wide range of views on codependency, everyone agrees that it is an unhealthy centering of one's life in another person. Whether that person is an addict or not does not seem to matter. Thus, the word *codependency* is applied today to a wide range of approval-seeking and people-pleasing behaviors. People who seek to impress others, people who have a "messiah complex," people who have low self-esteem — all are being called codependents. Sharon Wegsheider-Cruse, a leading writer on this topic, defines codependency as "a treatable disease characterized by preoccupation as well as groups of extreme dependencies on other persons (emotionally, socially, sometimes physically) or substances (such as alcohol, drugs, nicotine, and sugar) and on behaviors (such as workaholism, gambling, and compulsive sexual acting-out)" (*The Counselor,* March/April 1990). For her, codependency is practically synonymous with dependency and addictive involvement.

In the absence of a national standard on the definition and characteristics of codependency, it is likely that this word will continue to be used to describe a variety of behaviors. I use it to refer to addictive relationships of all kinds — whether with addicts or others. Having counseled with many codependents and observed their suffering firsthand, I take this disease very seriously and know from personal experience how difficult it is to break free of it. Therefore, I will continue in this book to speak of codependency as an addiction and not merely a bad habit.

Just as many people who drink do so abusively at times but do not become alcoholics, many people demonstrate codependent behaviors at times without becoming codependents. Obviously, then, I emphatically disagree with Sharon Wegsheider-Cruse and others who maintain that the overwhelming majority of people in our culture are codependents. This is not even true for members of alcoholic families! The term codependency is trivialized and made meaningless when it is applied to everyone who, at some time or other, demonstrates approval-seeking and people-pleasing behavior. Most people can stop doing this rather easily; codependents cannot.

Nevertheless, I am glad that the term codependency has escaped its previous exclusive association with chemical dependency. Many codependents are suffering in other contexts. Expanding the metaphor to include all addictive relationships can help these suffering people recognize their predicament and avail themselves of the various Twelve Step fellowships (for instance, Al-Anon, Co-Dependents Anonymous, Adult Children of Alcoholics) that can help them find their way to new life. This is a most welcome development indeed!

CHAPTER TWO
The Shame Game

Whenever I present lectures and workshops on codependency, someone invariably asks if certain people are more vulnerable to codependency than others. I answer the question with a qualified "yes." People who carry unresolved developmental issues from childhood are at a high risk for codependency. However, even healthy people living in an emotionally demanding environment can become codependent. In *Lost in the Shuffle,* Robert Subby speaks of "early-onset" versus "late-onset" codependency. Early-onset codependency begins developing during the childhood years, while late-onset codependency happens during the adult years. The problem for early-onsetters is that as adults they actually create the emotionally demanding circumstances that lead to the progression of their addiction. They do this largely as a result of poor communication.

Troubled Families

Researchers have learned a great deal during the past few decades about the importance of family. We now know, for example, that families are systems — that they have a kind of life of their own and that everyone in a family participates in that life. What makes the family system a healthy or unhealthy environment are the rules that govern the behavior of people in that system. In a healthy family system, the rules are reasonable and conducive to growth; they help individuals experience a vibrant sense of life in the family. In troubled families, where there is alcoholism, work addiction, or other problems, the rules operative in the family system often negate life and growth. A few characteristics of troubled families are described below.

1. *There are many covert rules.* Expectations are communicated indirectly, nonverbally. Family members are expected to know what they are supposed to do. Angry glares and frustrated sighs are the language that informs them.

2. *People do not feel free to talk about their feelings openly.* It is considered wrong to have certain feelings.

3. *There are many "secrets,"* no-talk areas that cannot be discussed. Addiction counselors like to say that it is as though there is a white elephant sitting in the living room, but no one mentions it.

4. *Rules are very rigid and often enforced through extreme punitive measures.*

5. *Individuals are often shamed* — for instance, given the message that they're no good.

6. *People feel tired, tense, and angry.* Family members often describe this as "walking on eggshells."

7. *The family tries to present a picture of "having it together" to the outside world.* Things change the moment they get home, however.

8. *Emotional bonding is through negative feelings.* Intimacy is of a negative type.

Troubled families are closed systems in that individuals exist for the family rather than vice versa. I once dated a young woman, Lucy, who came from an extremely dysfunctional family. Everything went well until we started getting serious. Then her family started working on her. Because I didn't fall into line with the family dynamics by becoming her father's "foster son," I was viewed as a threat by the family. Their plans for Lucy didn't match what she and I had been dreaming about, but she was simply too weak to make the break at that time. Dysfunctional families are very hard to leave; some people never leave them.

Traditionally, addiction counselors have spoken of troubled families in the context of chemical dependency. These families are certainly dysfunctional. However, many other families demonstrate the eight characteristics described above. The focus of the problem may be chemical dependency, but it might just as well happen around work addiction; a prolonged illness; religious addiction; or an angry, rigid personality disorder of some kind. After all, it is not the drinking or drugging in itself that is the problem but the *behavior* that results from substance abuse. This behavior can be observed in many other contexts besides alcohol addiction.

Whenever we find troubled families, we also find people taking on certain roles to survive emotionally and spiritually. These roles are described below.

1. *The Counterdependent.* This is the person who uses the codependent as an enabler for his or her neurosis or addiction to alcohol, work, religion, and so on. The Counterdependent often comes across as angry, moralizing, lecturing, and punitive.

2. *The Caretaker.* This is codependency as a primary addiction. In dysfunctional families, the Caretaker often functions as an enabler of the Counterdependent and a bridge ("switchboard") between the Counterdependent and the children. This is an exhausting role. Caretakers often take on secondary addictions to food, shopping, television, and mood-altering chemicals to keep themselves functioning.

3. *The Hero.* Typically the oldest child, this person provides a sense of self-worth for the family through achievement. Heroes look good to society. They make good grades, chair our committees, run our churches. Mom and Dad can focus on this person and say, "We must be doing something right." However, Heroes, like everyone else in this family, feel lonely, resentful, worthless, and fearful inside. They also get trapped in the role of earning positive attention by impressing others, which sets them up as prime candidates for work addiction or caretaking. It is typical of a Hero to say, "I'll never drink like my dad," then marry an alcoholic.

4. *The Lost Child.* This person learns to "fade into the woodwork" by being average and unobtrusive. "Don't make waves" is the Lost Child's motto. Living in a dysfunctional family is frightening, and Lost Children cope by repressing feelings and withdrawing. In a group they seem to "disappear." They pay a high price, however, for these repressed feelings often move them to intense depression, suicidal tendencies, overeating, and chemical dependency. Mom and Dad look at this kid and say, "At least we don't have to worry about that one."

5. *The Scapegoat.* Every dysfunctional family has its "black sheep," for the family dynamics require it. This person learns early in life that negative attention is better than no attention at all so he or she is constantly testing the rules and getting into trouble. Scapegoats often have problems in school, hang out with the "wrong crowd," and become chemically dependent and/or pregnant at an early age. "What are we going to do with this kid?" Mom and Dad lament. In many ways, however, this person is the healthiest in the family because her or his behavior and feelings, while troubled, at least agree.

6. *The Mascot.* Typically the youngest, this is the "family pet." Mascots bring diversion to the family through clowning, humor, being cute, and changing the subject. They are the ones who learn (and remember!) hundreds of jokes, which they are pleased to recite at any time. No one takes this person seriously, however. The family tries hard to "hide the truth so as not to upset her or him," but the Mascot knows there is something going on. Mascots have all the feelings but none of the facts, a crazy-making situation. Like everyone else in this family, Mascots are at a high risk for chemical dependency and other addictions.

In families where there are fewer than four children, it is possible to see a blending of roles — a Hero/Lost Child or a Mascot/Scapegoat, for example. Also, we need to acknowledge that these roles are evidenced to some degree in almost all families. The difference is that in healthy, open families, individuals can move in and out of these roles as the situation requires. In troubled families they get stuck in these roles. That's what all the interest in ACOA is about: people trying to get unstuck from the roles they put on during childhood. It makes a lot of sense to put on a suit of armor when you're in a war, but a suit of armor is a positive nuisance when you're trying to hug someone.

From my experience as a therapist working with troubled families, I attest to how well these roles describe the dynamics of such families. Time after time the same people seemed to be showing up for Family Week. They varied widely in race, creed, wealth, and intelligence, but their family dynamics were the same. When these roles and family dynamics were explained to them, they were able to recognize themselves and one another and to begin working on their own recovery.

Everyone in a troubled family is hurting. They are not all caretakers; some may even be manifesting counterdependent tendencies because of their movement into other addictions. Even counterdependents such as alcoholics and work addicts, however, will eventually come to a time in recovery when they must deal with their deeper dependency tendencies.

Communicating Shame

Everyone who lives in a troubled family has the experience of being loved conditionally: "I am loved, accepted, or approved because....I am not loved for who I am (or simply because I am) but for what I can do." This realization naturally fosters a utilitarian view of the self-concept: "I must *do* that which will bring me acceptance, love, and approval." People with this internal programming do not experience themselves as good and lovable. They believe that it is by doing the right things that one gains love, acceptance, and approval from others. Without this approval, they cannot experience self-acceptance. This is the "program" out of which the approval-seeking behavior of codependents arises.

We are not talking here about "our basic humanity" or "normal human development." Conditional love is common, but that does not make it normal. It is sick!

Healthy human development (especially among children) proceeds through stages in which self-validation depends on the validation of others. In a dysfunctional environment, this validation is conditional, inconsistent, and sometimes even neglected. It is also bracketed by terms of approval and disapproval.

Validation, one of the most important factors for growth, means simply reflecting for others (or even ourselves) the reality that we perceive. A validating mother says to her angry child, "I see you are angry about this; it's okay for you to be angry." She then might go on to help the child find constructive ways to express anger. This validation helps the child to say internally, "I *do* feel something; my feeling is real, and it is called anger." There is a mountain of research indicating that everyone needs this kind of validation.

In a dysfunctional environment, there is little validation, and much invalidation. If the child is angry, Mother might invalidate by doing the following:

1. *Ignoring the feeling.* For the child, the message is "You don't feel anything." This is a real crazy-maker.

2. *Negating the feeling.* Mother says, "Don't be angry!" or "That's nothing to get angry about." For the child the message is "I shouldn't have this feeling."

3. *Judging the feeling.* Mother says, "Big boys (or girls) don't get mad about this." Now it is a bad thing to have this feeling.

4. *Giving advice.* Actually, this is a way of ignoring the feeling. Mother goes to the angry child and skips the step of validation by giving advice on what to do when he or she gets angry.

Almost everyone in our society experienced invalidation as a child, not from any ill will on the part of our parents but because of their ignorance of human development and communication skills. Consequently, most of us learned that it was wrong to have certain feelings. Many learned that it was wrong to be angry or wrong to cry when sad or wrong to have sexual feelings. With this programming, *we judge ourselves as bad people because we have these feelings.* Our only solution is to repress them or ignore their existence in our consciousness. By doing this, we send them into the unconscious, where they live a life of their own and later make us sick in many ways — one of which is codependency.

In addition to invalidating feelings (and thoughts, dreams, and so on), the dysfunctional environment features approval and disapproval. Father says to his young daughter, "Make Daddy proud of you and eat all your food." Poor little soul! What if she's not hungry? Will Daddy still approve of her? Better not take a chance. She eats it all, planting in her unconscious the seeds of compulsive overeating.

Of course, no parent intends to do harm. Father just wants his daughter to be well nourished. Through the years, he makes the same mistake again and again, telling his daughter in so many ways that he disapproves of her for her behavior. She brings home a report card with all A's and one B, and he criticizes her for the B. Sometimes when he is angry about her behavior, he calls her names like "Brat" and "Stupid." He compares her constantly with her older sister, whom she grows to hate through the years.

The dynamic of approval/disapproval is a subtle one. Parents do not need to disapprove explicitly of their children to hurt them with it. All Mother has to do is say, "Be a good boy and don't get Mommy angry today," and the setup is there. One is a good boy if one does not get Mommy angry. The problem is, how does one do *that*? Mother doesn't realize that she has made her son responsible for her emotional life and that he will later feel guilty when she becomes angry — even if her anger has nothing to do with his behavior. Codependents feel responsible for other people's feelings, even if they did nothing to influence those feelings. Thus, we see that this dynamic is programmed through approval/disapproval.

As a result of years of invalidation, approval, and disapproval, children grow up feeling conditionally loved. The emotional scar from this is inner shame, the conviction that "I'm no good in myself" or "I'm only good for what I can do." Everybody has this, although some much more than others. To the degree to which we experienced invalidation and disapproval, there will be more or less inner shame.

While it is true that the most important environment is the home, we need to acknowledge the importance of other environments. Invalidation, approval, and disapproval happen in schools, churches, and the workplace. Even with a perfect home life (and there are none of these), it is possible to be significantly scarred by other relatives, teachers, playmates, and ministers. Moreover, shaming hurts not only children but adolescents and adults as well. If we experience much shame from childhood, it will carry over into adolescence and adulthood. Even with a healthy childhood, however, a shaming environment can create enough problems to move a healthy adult into codependency. This is especially true if the adult has poor relational and spiritual-living skills.

Clients often ask why people do all this shaming and invalidating. Surely, part of the problem is that we just haven't learned another way to communicate; we're just expressing frustrations in the way we saw others do it. The payoff, however, needs to be underscored: *Invalidation, approval, and disapproval often are used to control people through the fear of rejection.* Having built shame into the consciousness of their children, parents can control them through approval and disapproval. "If you do what I say, I will give you my approval. If not, I just might shame you."

The dynamics of shame and control carry over into the school, workplace, and into the Church. Shame-based people can be controlled by giving them approval for certain behaviors and disapproval for others. The approval and disapproval might be awarded in the form of a grade, a raise, a guarantee of redemptive grace, or something as simple as a smile. Almost anything can become a medium for communicating approval and disapproval. This dynamic moves us to look outside ourselves for acceptance and validation; this act of external-referencing is the essence of addiction.

While reading Anne Wilson Schaef's book *When Society Becomes an Addict,* it occurred to me that much of the entire social system in which we live operates out of shame and approval. In later chapters we will reflect more deeply upon this.

Codependent Programming

The experience of being loved conditionally leaves a sense of emotional worthlessness that translates mentally into "I'm no good" or "I'm no good unless I do the right things." Everyone has some of this programming, some more than others. This is a painful state, so it is only natural for the psyche to try to correct this distortion. If this correction is worked out in the same dysfunctional environment that produced the pain, the result will be further distortion.

The self-concept that emerges out of shame is essentially utilitarian — that is, it tries to identify itself as good because it can *do something* or because it is *identified with* something that is good. It is external-referenced — dependent on things outside itself for validation. People in this state believe that other people and circumstances are responsible for the way they feel. They have no control over their emotional life — except to the extent they can succeed in controlling other people and circumstances. And this is precisely what they try to do: *control other people and circumstances.* The logic is impeccable: "If other people and circumstances can give me pain, then I must control these people and circumstances so they no longer give me pain."

And how, pray tell, do we control other people and circumstances?

That's easy! We give or withhold approval. "If you hurt me, I will hurt you; if you're nice to me, I'll be nice to you" is the game. It's how *our* buttons get pushed; why not others'?

Another dysfunctional strategy for correcting inner shame is *perfectionism*. Again the logic is compelling: "If I'm no good because I do things the wrong way, then the way I can become good is by doing things the perfect way." In Christianity this is called salvation by good works, and everybody practices it to some degree. Extremely perfectionistic people give approval only if something is done perfectly. Consequently, they are very hard on themselves and others. They are impatient, intolerant, and often procrastinate in performing tasks or finishing projects (so they don't get evaluated). As parents, they make their children miserable; no matter what the kids do, it is never good enough. This attitude can also be found in schools, businesses, and in the Church.

Perfectionistic people also have difficulty accepting correction or unpleasant feedback. When confronted, they quickly become defensive and begin doling out large servings of disapproval to try to control the other person into leaving them alone. To them, imperfection means being no good as a person. It's all about their inner shame.

Because the self-concept of a shame-based person becomes strongly identified with things outside the self, the perfectionism of these people carries over to these identifications. For example, if I strongly identify with a football team or a particular church, then you'd better not criticize these. I will experience any such criticism of my country, my school, my church, or my team as criticism of my self. People actually come to blows about such matters, a situation due to perfectionistic identifications.

Perfectionism and control: these are the two most common ways people attempt to compensate for inner shame. As the chart on page 31 illustrates, there are additional compensations sought by codependents and counterdependents, but it is important to see that both groups have very much in common.

ADDICTION: The Big Picture

DEVELOPMENTAL ENVIRONMENT
Family, Work, School, Church, Society

Dysfunctional   Invalidation   Approval/Disapproval
Communication

Conditional Love: "You're no good unless…."

INNER SHAME
("I'm no good!")

Compensatory Response
("But I'll be okay when….")
   A. "…I am perfect."
   B. "…I am in control."

C. "…others are impressed with me."   D. "…I don't need anyone."
(Codependent response)   *(Counterdependent response)*
1. When others approve of me, it   1. If I let myself need people,
   means I am okay.   they will be able to hurt me.
2. If I do what impresses others, they 2. If I give in to others, they will
   will approve of me.   think I am weak.
3. I must not upset others.   3. If you don't look out for num-
4. Others' needs are more important   ber one, then who will?
   than my own.

Addictions Caretaking Messianism Chemical Dependency Gambling
         Food Relationships Work Money
      Shopping Worrying Religion Sex Television

Dysfunctional   Invalidation   Approval/Disapproval
Communication
      Create unhealthy developmental environment for others

The counterdependent stance toward shame is to strive for a *thoroughgoing independence and autonomy*. "I don't need people! People will only hurt me if I allow myself to need them" is their position. Therefore, counterdependents undertake strategies in control and perfectionism that isolate them from others. They are self-righteous, grandiose, condescending, patronizing, and very angry. It must be their way or no way. They are also selfish, controlling, and narcissistic. Naturally, these attitudes keep other people at arm's length. Counterdependents are lonely people. This loneliness, added to their shame and anger, increases their experience of emotional pain. Consequently, they frequently use alcohol/drugs, gambling, work, and other addictions to numb their pain.

Codependents take a different approach to correcting shame. "If I'm no good because others disapprove of me, then I must find ways to get them to approve of me." This is the origin of the people-pleasing and approval-seeking behavior we have discussed. We understand now that this behavior arises from an attempt to compensate for inner shame. In addition to seeking approval, codependents are also highly controlling and perfectionistic. Unlike counterdependents, however, codependents enlist these two strategies in the service of gaining approval or minimizing disapproval ("I must not upset others").

Relational Patterns

There are very few pure codependents or counterdependents in our culture. Most of us carry elements of both. When we find ourselves in an environment where one side is emphasized, it is common to react by going the other way. If our spouse becomes counterdependent, we become codependent.

It is often said that opposites attract, and never is this more obvious than when a codependent is focused on gaining approval from a counterdependent. This is usually the case with alcoholics (who are usually counterdependent) and their spouses (who are codependent). When both are into their addictions, the dance of shame between them moves them deeper into their addictions. The more she drinks, the more he caretakes her and the kids to gain her approval and minimize her disapproval; the more he caretakes, the more she drinks. These addictions feed off each other.

The same dynamic appears in a work environment that values people for what they can do rather than for who they are. Given a human being who already carries a little shame within, who needs money to survive, and who does not perceive himself to have many options in the workplace, it is natural that this person would assume a codependent attitude toward the boss or job. He begins to "brown-nose," to swallow his pride, and to live in fear that his income will be taken away.

So institutions often function as counterdependents, saying in effect, "If you don't like the way we do things here, go work someplace else!" This message, of course, generates codependent responses from employees. Approval and disapproval are meted out with raises or cuts in pay, promotions and demotions, retirement benefits and firings. This is the way of the world, of course. It is also how so many of us got sick. Frequently, a man or woman who has to act as a codependent at work will compensate by acting as a counterdependent at home, bossing people around, drinking heavily, and so on. The dance of shame takes expression in many patterns.

When two codependents become focused on each other, the result is a pattern of relationship called "enmeshment." They are like two cards leaning against each other; pull one away, the other falls flat. They *need* each other! In their minds, this neediness is proof of their love. Our society and its love (codependency) songs reassure them that people who need people are the luckiest people in the world.

Lest the reader misunderstand enmeshment, it must be said here that *people do need people.* We cannot meet our needs in isolation.

The problem with enmeshments is the overwhelming need for one another's constant approval and reassurance. "Because you need my approval, I have security in the relationship" is the position here. Enmeshed people are constantly reacting to one another in approval and disapproval. They hold power over one another, and this in itself is an addictive dynamic. Sad to say, it is also what passes for love in the minds of many people.

Spreading the Bad News

Codependents are hooked on a drug called approval. If they get this drug from other people, they feel they are okay. The people who give them this drug are also okay — good people!

What if people do not give this approval? At this point, healthy people can turn inward and reassure themselves that they are okay. Not codependents, however. Their addiction blocks the way to self-validation; instead, they depend upon the approval of others for self-validation. When, for whatever reason, the other does not supply the approval drug in the manner desired, the codependent quickly judges that person as uncaring, insensitive, and mean. If the codependent is tied to the other person through family or work, then he or she will begin to search for ways to gain this approval.

One strategy for gaining approval is *out-competing* with the other. In this way the disapproval of the other will be shown to have arisen from an "inferior" human being, thus lessening its sting. Hence, a younger sibling will try to bring home better grades to "rise above" the disapproval of an older sibling. A wife will join the work force and try to earn more money than her disapproving husband. Coaches and supervisors have been known to reward "one-upmanship" to stimulate greater efforts. This kind of competitiveness is destructive, however, for it keeps people in a comparing mode and hence, external-referenced. It is really about controlling people through shaming.

When, as often happens, it turns out that we cannot out-compete the disapproving one, we can resort to *trashing.* This is a second, all-too-common, codependent response. In trashing another, we focus on his or her negative traits; we talk about these with others (gossiping); we judge the person's motives for doing what he or she does; we focus on convincing ourselves and others that the disapproving one is a bad person. "Who wants approval from a bad person anyway?" we conclude. In this manner, codependents discount any kind of information that shows them in a disapproving light.

A third way codependents respond to the disapproval of others is through *people-pleasing behavior.* If we decide that the approval of other people is necessary for our well-being, we must find ways to turn their disapproval into approval. We do things we hope will please them so they will become grateful to us and give us our drug. This is how we become addicted to caretaking.

There is nothing wrong with performing good deeds for others, of course. For codependents, however, the focus is not really on the good deed. It is getting approval that matters. This brings a certain egocentricity into the "altruism" of the codependent. "I'm doing it for you, for me" is the truth about people-pleasing. Furthermore, this people-pleasing strategy often moves the codependent into behaviors that compromise his or her values. This is especially true in the area of sexuality, where codependents will frequently give in to make the other happy.

A fourth response, closely related to people-pleasing, is *conflict-avoidance behavior.* When it seems unlikely that the one from whom we seek approval will give it to us, the best we can do is avoid provoking his or her disapproval. Therefore, we make a commitment to avoid upsetting him or her. This is problem enough, but many codependents go much further, attempting to prevent other people and circumstances from upsetting the object of their focus. Here we find the root from which the controlling behavior of codependency arises. And again we see that its focus is in gaining approval.

A fifth codependent strategy for coping with disapproval is *trying to impress other people.* Maybe if the disapproving one could see that other people think we are wonderful, then he or she would come around too. Entire careers have been fueled by this motivation! For example, the wife who is popular among her working colleagues may be hoping all the while that her disapproving husband will see that she is really a great woman.

An even more common example is the man or woman from a troubled home who achieves considerable career success, hoping finally to gain the approval of his or her disapproving parents. This dynamic is especially common among those operating out of the Hero role in their families. They often go on to develop that intriguing species of codependency called Messianism. Messiahs work hard, often as helping professionals (nurses, teachers, ministers, and so on), but the payoff that moves them to do what they do is approval.

Summary of Addictive Dynamics

Most of us experienced conditional love in our developmental environments, both by observing the experiences of others and through feeling their approval or disapproval. To the degree that we experience conditional love, we also experience inner shame, the emotional conviction that we're no good. With this shame comes anxiety, guilt, and the building of a defensive ego that keeps us trapped in loneliness.

People commonly attempt to compensate for inner shame by trying to control and manipulate that which hurts them. Perfectionism is another common way to try to stave off disapproval from others. In addition, counterdependents cultivate an autonomy that negates their need for belonging, while codependent responses emphasize approval-seeking and people-pleasing behavior. The responses of both counterdependents and codependents produce short-term relief but long-term pain. Consequently, people operating out of these dynamics inevitably become involved in a variety of addictions to numb their emotional pain. These addictions keep them locked in pain, however, and perpetuate an environment in which they pass on their inner shame to others through invalidation, approval, and disapproval.

Checklist of Codependent Behaviors

How much do you identify with the characteristics listed below?
-2 Strongly Disagree   -1 Disagree   0 Not Sure
+1 Agree   +2 Strongly Agree

-2	-1	0	+1	+2

1. I have difficulty saying "no" when people ask me to do something, even when I know I should not do it.
2. I feel responsible for problems with others and the world that I did not cause.
3. I have a hard time being good to myself. It feels so selfish!
4. I put others' needs before my own, even when their needs are not urgent and mine are.
5. When other people give me approval, it helps me to accept myself.
6. When other people criticize something I do, I feel like a failure.
7. I put off doing or saying things that upset people to avoid "making a scene."
8. In the areas of my life where I experience approval, I often become overinvolved.
9. If something I do is not done perfectly, I become impatient.

10. When others point out an imperfection in me, I become defensive.
11. If I am not in control of a situation or project, I feel panicky.
12. I frequently compare myself with other people to see if I'm okay.
13. When I'm around other people who seem to "have it together," I feel inadequate.
14. Deep down inside, I don't really like myself, and I hide this from others.
15. When I feel upset, I tend to blame and criticize people and circumstances for my feelings.
16. I have a difficult time getting myself out of unhealthy relationships with others.
17. I sometimes compromise my values to stay in unhealthy relationships with others.
18. I have a difficult time asking people to help me do things I cannot do myself.
19. I often feel burdened with the attitude "If I don't do it, no one else will."
20. My first reaction to a suggestion to try something new is usually negative.

-5 — +5 Early-stage codependency
+6 — +12 Mid-stage codependency
+13 — Above chronic codependency

CHAPTER THREE
The First Steps
to Recovery

The disease of alcoholism is often difficult for those who are not alcoholics to understand. "Why can't they see how destructive their drinking has become!" we lament. "Why don't they just stop?"

It is the same with codependency. We ask, "Why don't they take better care of themselves? Why can't they see how damaging their enabling and controlling behavior has become?"

Addiction is an insidious disease process. The deeper a person goes into the disease, the less insight and will power he or she has, becoming sincerely deluded about a wide range of issues. Alcoholics who are losing everything still believe they can control their drinking; codependents still believe they can fix everything for everyone — even while the "ship" is sinking.

There is a way out of the addictive process. It is not the way of will power but the way of surrender. As long as the addict maintains the delusion of being in control, there is no hope for recovery. Although many nonaddicts believe that the solution lies in exerting will power — in "getting a grip" by making up one's mind to never indulge the fix again — in reality just the opposite is true. The only way out of an addiction is to "throw in the towel," to admit defeat, and then to become open to another way of living. That is what the Twelve Steps teach us to do.

The First Step

We admitted we were powerless over controlling other people — that our lives had become unmanageable.

The above statement is an adaptation of the First Step of Alcoholics Anonymous. It is the key to recovery. If the addict does not work this step, no real healing can take place.

I am increasingly impressed by the wisdom of the Twelve Steps. The First Step in particular is a real gem, for it minces no words in getting to the crux of the matter. It recognizes that the center around which the consciousness of codependents turns is another person (or people) and invites the codependent to see how living out of this center has made him or her miserable. It confronts the denial and delusion of the addict by saying, "You aren't in control, and you are hurting yourself and others with your behavior." No practicing addict wants to hear this; addiction feeds on contrary beliefs.

Many people consider the First Step to be rather rough, especially on codependents. "Why don't we ease gently into recovery?" they ask. "Why start on such a negative note?"

This objection misses the point, which is that addiction is an ugly, destructive, and insidious disease process. Half-measures do not succeed in helping recovery. The heart of the matter is that the codependent has become spiritually centered on something or someone, and this situation has brought destruction to this person and others. The nature of this false center must be pointed out; to tiptoe around it leaves the false center — and hence the addiction — perfectly intact. The false center must be given up if the addict is ever to enter the recovery process. If the false center is not rejected, he or she remains an addict.

If after completing the Checklist of Codependent Behaviors at the end of Chapter Two, you feel you have a problem with codependency, you need to familiarize yourself with the three things that are necessary before you can be freed from an addictive center.

First, you must give up the addictive fix. The alcoholic must stop drinking; the gambler must stop gambling; the overeater must stop overeating; the codependent must give up the relationship.

In saying that a codependent must give up the relationship, I do not mean that a codependent spouse must get a divorce or that a parent must kick the addicted child out of the home. You can remain in codependency even if the other moves away. What you must give up is not the other person but the effort to *control* the other person. This means that you must give up all enabling, rescuing, caretaking, people-pleasing, approval-seeking, and other manipulative behavior. You must detach from the other person and allow him or her to experience the consequences of his or her behavior — even if pain is one of the consequences. This pain may very well be a catalyst to that person's own recovery.

Detaching from the person you are centered on will not be easy, for you will probably continue to see this person frequently. The alcoholic can continue living without alcohol; but for the recovering codependent, a relationship with the person on whom he or she was codependently focused is often necessary. Therefore, you will do well to become involved in a support group such as Al-Anon, Co-Dependents Anonymous, or Adult Children of Alcoholics. Such groups can support you in your effort to give up controlling others.

Giving up control does not mean giving up care. Neither does it mean that you cease to help others. You cannot help caring, but the manner in which you express your care must leave the other free. You must consciously ask, "Am I helping or am I trying to control?" Appendix Two provides some guidance in discerning the difference. Your support group can also be helpful.

The second thing you must do to free yourself from codependency is recognize your powerlessness over others.

To reinforce your resolve to give up controlling others, it is helpful to see that your efforts to control them were largely unsuccessful anyway. Take an honest look at what happened. Did all your efforts to control ever accomplish much more than a band-aid fix?

We control almost nothing in life. The only thing we have ultimate control over is our attitude about what is happening to us. Everything else — health, prosperity, children, property, and so on — is on loan and can be lost in an instant.

If this is true about life, it is certainly true in our relationships with others. We cannot control others — certainly not their attitudes about us. We cannot make people like us if they do not want to like us. Furthermore, all our efforts to control and impress them only make them like us less.

Control is not a Christian value. Being in control is not a spiritual ideal. Facing this truth is hard, but living with the illusion of control is harder. In the end the truth will set you free, and the truth is that you cannot control the behavior of anyone but yourself.

Spend a few minutes thinking about that. Jot down a few notes about the ways you have tried to control others. See how futile the effort has been. Let this awareness deepen your resolve to give up control.

Finally, to gain freedom from codependency, you must see how your effort to control others has made your life unmanageable. What have you given up to stay in a relationship with the person you are so focused upon? What hobbies have you neglected? What books have you not read? What friendships have you put on a back burner? What spiritual disciplines have gone undone? These are among the most costly of consequences, for it is in giving up these things that you give away yourself. When you give up activities and values that previously were important to you to stay in a relationship, your life becomes unbalanced and you lose touch with your own wants and needs.

Of course, there are other consequences to face as well. How much time do you spend each day thinking about your relationship with the other? How much time do you spend worrying? How many sleepless nights do you have? How many NOW-moments with their surprises go unseen? How much anger and resentment do you feel? How many ways have you compromised your values to stay in this relationship? How much abuse have you taken from the other person? What other addictions (eating, sex, work, religion) have you gotten into since entering this relationship? How much physical sickness have you endured because your body has become weak?

Seriously considering these questions can help you see how codependency has affected your life. They deserve your time and consideration. Write down your responses to each of them and see how many ways being codependently focused on another has hurt you. Let this recognition deepen your resolve to give up the unhealthy relationship and begin learning a new way to care for others.

If you make an honest effort to work the First Step, you will begin to feel a sense of relief. You will not be out of the storm yet, but you will surely be on the way out. This knowledge in itself will give you a sense of serenity.

The Second Step

Came to believe that a Power greater than ourselves could restore us to sanity.

This is the second of AA's Twelve Steps, but it can work quite well for codependents in recovery.

If you work Step One honestly, you will come to an experience of profound ego-deflation, for all your long-cultivated delusions about controlling others and yourself will be burst. Step One is a necessary step, but it is certainly not a pleasant one. Its almost brutal frankness can leave you feeling relieved that the mind games you have been playing have ended, but it can also leave you feeling humiliated and depressed. That's where Step Two comes in.

Step Two is an affirmation of hope. It states that things can get better. You can recover your sanity; your mind can behave according to the dictates of reason rather than emotional compulsion. For this to happen, however, you will have to believe in a Power greater than yourself. This requirement is a stumbling block for many people.

To some, the term *Higher Power,* as used in the context of Step Two, refers to God in a religious sense. Others, however, have serious difficulties with religious language. Some people have suffered abuse from rigid, religiously addicted parents, teachers, and ministers; others have simply had no religious education and haven't developed any sense of what a relationship with God might be like.

You will have to search out the meaning of Higher Power in your own way. Recovery is about embracing your own spiritual journey, and this means struggling with all your questions about God, religion, church, and so on.

Regardless of your religious convictions, however, do not make the mistake of limiting the concept of a Higher Power to specifically religious concerns. In the language of Step Two, a Higher Power is anything that helps restore sanity. Such Powers abound everywhere and might include

- the wisdom and encouragement of a support group,
- a faithful, loving spouse,
- a good friend,
- an employer who holds you accountable for doing good work,
- the criminal justice system that holds you accountable for illegal actions,
- a singing mockingbird that helps you hear something other than internal anxiety,
- an exercise program that strengthens the body.

Remember, sanity is living by reason rather than emotional compulsion. Anything that helps you live a life free from emotional compulsion is the work of the Higher Power.

In working Step Two, you must commit to using resources that can help you live a life of sanity. You must spend less time around people and places that bring forth an insane, addictive response from you. "You must change playgrounds and playmates," says AA. And on the positive side, you must choose healthy playgrounds and playmates.

One of the best ways to work Step Two, then, is to spend time in fellowship with others who are experienced in recovery. Their living presence is a sign of hope; if they could make it, you can too. Things don't have to be crazy like they once were. There is another way to live, and there are many ways the Higher Power helps us become the people we were created to be. That's good news indeed!

Step Three

Made a decision to turn our will and our lives over to the care of God as we understood Him.

This is the step of surrender. Those who truly work this step will find serenity.

Step Two teaches you to be hopeful by recognizing the many resources that move you toward sanity. In many ways, Step Two is an intellectual affirmation, a mental surrender, and this is important. If the intellect is not convinced, no lasting surrender of the will is possible.

Nevertheless, a surrender of the intellect does not of itself lead you to a surrender of the will. There are many brilliant theologians in the Church today, but how many living saints? Although informed and directed by intellect, the life of the will is of a different energy dynamism than that of the intellect. Therefore, a surrender on the level of will is necessary, and that is what Step Three is about.

Before going on to discuss the practical working of Step Three, it will be helpful to recognize that it is at the level of will that you are caught in the addictive process. No addict intellectually approves of his or her addictive behavior. If recovery were dependent on intellectual exertion alone, we would have no addicts. The predicament in which addicts find themselves was best described by Saint Paul in Romans 7:15-24.

What I do, I do not understand. For I do not do what I want, but I do what I hate. Now if I do what I do not want, I concur that the law is good. So now it is no longer I who do it, but sin that dwells in me. For I know that good does not dwell in me, that is, in my flesh. The willing is ready at hand, but doing the good is not. For I do not do the good I want, but I do the evil I do not want. Now if [I] do what I do not want, it is no longer I who do it, but sin that dwells in me. So, then, I discover the principle that when I want to do right, evil is at hand. For I take delight in the law of God, in my inner self, but I see in my members another principle at war with the law of my mind, taking me captive to the law of sin that dwells in my members. Miserable one that I am! Who will deliver me from this mortal body?

No better description of the spiritual predicament addicts find themselves in has ever been written. Of course, Paul uses the word *sin* where, in this context, we would say *addiction,* but it is exactly the same experience. I think Saint Paul would not hesitate to call alcoholism and codependency sin-diseases. They are of the sin-power because they lead us to do evil deeds; they are diseases because we are powerless to rid ourselves of them through the exercise of intellectual volition.

In response to Saint Paul's question, "Who will deliver me from this mortal body?" we affirm, on an intellectual level, that our Higher Power can do this. Now comes the next question — the hardest of all: Will you let your Higher Power free you? Do you really want to give up living a life of self-will? Now we are talking about spiritual issues.

Step Three is an invitation to begin doing what we need to do and not what we want to do. It means giving up self-will and control so we may begin growing in directions we cannot predict. This is exciting, but it is also frightening. Exciting because we know we are finally on the road that leads to true happiness; frightening because we do not know where this road leads or what kind of persons we will turn out to be. These fears are normal, but they need to be faced. To avoid discussing them is to allow fear a foothold, a movement toward addiction. In the end there is nothing to do but to take this new road, for we know from Step One where the other way goes.

You do not have to like Step Three to benefit from it. In the program we emphasize walking the walk and not talking the talk. On a practical level this slogan means that we begin doing what we need to do to take care of ourselves, even when we do not feel like doing it. Eventually, a new emotional system will bring consolation to support these healthy choices; but in the early stages, we will surely experience much emotional resistance. This resistance to doing what is good is addiction calling us to relapse. By offering ourselves to the care of God in prayer, we can always find the strength to overcome this resistance. Calling a supportive friend or family member is another way to receive strength.

For the Christian in recovery, Step Three means recognizing that you belong to Christ. You are a human cell in his Mystical Body. To live by the life of his Body is to become the person he has created you to be — a branch on his vine. It is to become your True Self.

Summary

In recovery from addiction, there are four R's that summarize the work to be done:

1. *Recognition* of the problem. This is what you learn from Step One.
2. *Recentering* your life. This is the movement of Steps Two, Three, and Eleven.
3. *Retraining* the manner in which you meet your needs. Steps Six and Seven address this issue.
4. *Resolving* emotional pain. Steps Four, Five, Eight, Nine, and Ten provide guidance for this work.

Although each of these four areas is essential for ongoing growth and integration, the first two — recognition and recentering — are the most important. As long as you are actively indulging a harmful addiction, it will be impossible to retrain consciousness or to resolve emotional pain. Counseling approaches that attempt to lead to retraining and healing without addressing addictions can provide short-term results, at best. If it is long-term health and growth that you hope for, however, recognizing your addictions and recentering your life on God as you understand him will also be necessary.

People who work Steps One through Three daily will find themselves naturally motivated to learn other ways to meet their needs. They will also feel themselves moved toward reconciliation with others. Without Steps One through Three, reconciliations usually are short-lived, for the addiction will continue to cause problems in relationships. Retraining alone will also bring poor results, for the addict's resolve to learn healthy new behavior will be overwhelmed by the compulsion to indulge old behavior.

The importance of recognizing your addictions and recentering your life in God cannot be overstated. No lasting growth is possible without this work. If you make a sincere effort in this direction, however, you will begin to experience serenity and a new joy in living, although many problems remain.

CHAPTER FOUR
Living Your Own Life

Codependency is a disease of lost selfhood. By taking care of others and staying preoccupied about our relationships, we lose touch with our own inner spontaneity. In the end we know perfectly well what the other wants, but we have no idea what we want (except, of course, that we want what the other wants).

How do we regain the self that has been lost? This is the question with which millions of people are struggling throughout the world.

In responding to this question, we begin by saying that working Steps One through Three of the Twelve Steps is the best way to begin the process of living your own life. Getting in touch with your Higher Power is also the best way to get in touch with your True Self. The God who lives within you is at one with your inner self; to experience God within is to experience yourself in the depths of your own being. There is really no experience of the True Self that can be separated from God, for God alone can reveal the deepest part of our being to our more superficial, conscious Ego.

Having discovered yourself in the mystery of God, there is, nevertheless, much left to learn. You must learn to share your feelings, to assert your needs, and to make decisions. In short, you must learn relationship skills. Furthermore, you must learn to relate according to the nature of your True Self and not according to the standards of others. If you do not learn these living skills, you will quickly return to living your life to please others and will lose the experience of being awake and alive within. That is why retraining the way you meet your needs is so important.

Rehabilitation Versus Habilitation

In counseling with codependents through the years, I have found that there are two types of people in recovery. First, there are those who once enjoyed a healthy sense of self but lost it after becoming enmeshed in a relationship with an unhealthy person. We might call this *late-onset codependency,* meaning that it began later in life. Such people can be rehabilitated, for they still possess certain memories, values, and convictions that have not been lost. Their healthy family upbringing proves itself a grace in recovery as they move quickly through the phases of recognition and recentering described in Chapter Three and begin learning new ways to care for themselves. They must continue to avoid enabling and other addictions, for they have entered the addictive process and can relapse just like anyone else. But once they begin recovery, they generally heal quickly, and they generally go through the retraining phase with great enthusiasm.

In contrast to these late-onset codependents are those who never received much care, affirmation, and teaching about living skills. These people suffer from *early-onset codependency,* for they have been acting codependently since childhood. Children of alcoholics and other addicts are prime examples of early-onset codependency. When they enter the recovery process as young adults or adults, they cannot be rehabilitated, for they were never habilitated (or made capable) in the first place. Instead, they must be habilitated, and this is no easy task. It is possible, however, as thousands of adult children of alcoholics throughout the country are demonstrating today.

Stages of Human Development

In speaking of habilitation, it will be helpful to review briefly the growth process. We come into this world knowing nothing except how to suck on a nipple and to cry when something is wrong with us. Everything else must be learned through the years. An awe-inspiring amount of learning goes on during the first few years of life. Before the age of four, the child learns how to speak, how to eat, how to get along with others, and many, many other lessons. Most of these lessons are assimilated from the environment through observation and imitation of others. Some, of course, are taught more formally. But there is no question that the behavior modeled by others — especially family members — serves as the most important source of education for our own behavior.

Although our growth unfolds in many directions, the dimension most relevant to this discussion on habilitation and rehabilitation concerns our social development — how we experience ourselves emotionally and relationally. The stages of social development have been studied by many authors, but the paradigm described by Erik Erikson continues to serve as a starting point for discussion. Erikson studied thousands of individuals from a variety of cultures and found a developmental pattern common to all. He summarized the primary issues and struggles that all must encounter during the process of social development as follows:

1. *Trust versus mistrust.* First two years of life.
2. *Autonomy versus shame.* Ages one to three years.
3. *Initiative versus guilt.* Ages three to six years.
4. *Industry versus inferiority.* Ages six to twelve years.
5. *Identity versus identity diffusion.* Ages twelve through eighteen years.
6. *Intimacy versus isolation.* Ages eighteen through thirty-three.
7. *Generativity [social awareness] versus self-absorption.* Ages thirty-three onward.
8. *Integrity versus despair.* Middle and old age.

According to Erikson, those who achieve a successful resolution of the issues of a growth stage are able to enter the next stage with more strength than those who do not achieve resolution. For example, infants and toddlers who learn through consistent care and attention that life is trustworthy will be more inclined to learn to be autonomous than those who are not properly loved. The latter will be more inclined to feel shameful or flawed inside.

Lists of characteristics of adult children of alcoholics bear a striking similarity to the consequences described by Erikson. ACOA's experience self-absorption, difficulties with intimacy, role confusion, inferiority, guilt, shame, and fear of abandonment. Although they have all attained partial resolution of the issues in each growth stage, the "leftover business" of the previous stages sabotages their efforts to grow in the present. This does not mean that ACOA's are mentally ill — only that they are developmentally hurting. This immaturity plus the emotional pain accumulated through the years contributes to early-onset codependency of ACOA's.

Erikson's stages also help us understand the differences between habilitating and rehabilitating people in recovery. In general, ACOA's need to be habilitated; they need to learn trust, autonomy, initiative, industry, identity, and intimacy. On the other hand, a person who had experienced healthy growth through the fifth stage could become codependent during the struggle for intimacy in the sixth stage. Such a late-onset codependent had already been habilitated and so would require a different program of recovery from an early-onset codependent. After dealing with the consequences of their addiction, late-onset codependents can generally move on with life. Early-onset codependents also need to deal with the consequences of their addiction, but *in addition* they need to learn what has been missed through the years.

Who will teach the early-onset codependent (henceforth called ACOA) the lessons missed? These lessons were not learned in the family of origin, so they must now be learned in the recovery group or family of choice. It is in this family of choice that ACOA's learn to re-parent themselves. Such re-parenting is an essential part of learning to live one's own life instead of living to please others.

Inner Child, Inner Parent

The first states of consciousness experienced by children are largely motivated by feelings. As a result of this, small children often act impulsively — as their feelings dictate. One of the most important tasks of parenting is to teach the child to discipline these impulses. It is a fine thing when the impulse is to play a creative game but quite another when the child wants to run into the street or to eat garbage. Inevitably, then, parents must begin to say, "No, don't do that!" to children even before they reach one year of age.

Throughout the early months and years, the external disciplining of the parent becomes part of the child's inner psychic process. The child begins to feel the boundaries set by parents checking her or his behavior internally. I recall, for example, a time when one of my own toddlers wandered over to a trash can, picked up the lid, and stood looking inside, shaking her head and saying, "No-no, no-no." She then wandered away from the trash, and I rejoiced that the process of internal disciplining was working.

By the age of four, a child already possesses an "internal parent" or Superego that serves to set boundaries for impulsive behavior. You can allow this child to play in the yard without the constant observation a fifteen-month-old would need. Four-year-olds still need external discipline (and will, even through the teenage years), but they already possess a capacity for internal discipline that makes parenting a great deal easier.

Many problems result, however, when children receive parenting that is extremely inconsistent, rigid, or harshly punitive. Two extreme outcomes are an overly rigid Superego or an overly permissive Superego. Both extremes lead to failures in social development. In the worst cases, the absence of internal discipline leads to sociopathic behavior, while the overly rigid types tend to become scrupulous and hyperaware.

Most ACOA's fall somewhere between these extremes. They usually received parenting that was inconsistent and often rigid and punitive at times and neglectful at other times. They were frequently emotionally invalidated, discounted, and shamed. The tactics of discipline tended to focus on approval and disapproval as described in Chapter Two.

As we get older, we do not lose our emotional, or Inner Child, level of experience; we simply grow layers around it. A problem for ACOA's and many others is that much about this Inner Child feels flawed or bad. In addition we retain elements of that first Superego into adulthood. For ACOA's the Superego is shaming, judgmental, and rigid (or for others, overly permissive). The dysfunctional dialogue that once took place between the Critical Parent and little child now continues between the Superego and Inner Child. No longer do our parents shame us; we do it to ourselves. No matter what we do, it is never good enough. Consequently, ACOA's frequently become perfectionistic and controlling in their efforts to gain external and internal approval.

How to Re-parent Yourself

One therapeutic model that is helping many codependents and ACOA's take charge of their own lives is transactional analysis (or TA). Writers such as Eric Berne *(Games People Play)* and Thomas Harris *(I'm O.K., You're O.K.),* who wrote about TA, state that most of us can identify at least three inner "voices," or psychic processes. Two of these voices, which we have already identified, are the Superego or Internal Parent (P) and the Inner Child (C). The third inner voice, and the most significant for this discussion, is the Adult (A).

The primary concerns of these three aspects of self are summarized on the next page.

Child — the feeling self and source of intuition, spontaneity, and creativity.

Parent — source of values and obligations.

Adult — source of rational guidance.

Each of these three levels can be both healthy and unhealthy. For example, we can speak of the Natural Child and the Wounded Child, the Nurturing Parent and the Critical Parent, the Enlightened Adult and the Ignorant Adult. These we can illustrate as below.

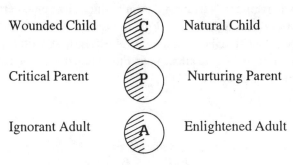

Wounded Child   **C**   Natural Child

Critical Parent   **P**   Nurturing Parent

Ignorant Adult   **A**   Enlightened Adult

By observing these inner states, we notice that at any given time we are acting out of one of them while the others are playing a secondary role. The illustration below demonstrates a person acting out of the Critical Parent state.

This Critical Parent may be speaking to another person or to his or her own inner states.

Once we begin to identify these inner states, we discover that

- Parent and Child have a close emotional relationship. Critical Parent and Wounded Child are bonded together through shame; Nurturing Parent and Natural Child are bonded together in love.

- Child and Adult are not emotionally close. Therefore, the Inner Child is little influenced by the Adult level.
- Parent and Adult relate through values and concepts. Therefore, a transformative dialogue is possible between Adult and Parent.

Given the above information, it becomes clear that the only way to heal the Wounded Child within is by taking the Critical Parent out of commission and activating the Nurturing Parent. The only way to activate the Nurturing Parent within is by empowering the Enlightened Adult. It is the role of the Enlightened Adult state to challenge the Critical Parent's rigid values and to substitute healthy values. In this way you allow your Enlightened Adult to run your life, as indicated below:

As an example of how all this might work, let us say that you made a mistake cooking a meal, and it has come out tasting terrible. Your company is ready to eat, and you are feeling embarrassed about it. In comes Critical Parent: "You blew it again! How many times have I told you that you just can't cook? Why did you have to pick such a hard recipe anyway? You can't do anything right!" All this internal self-judgment activates the Wounded Child. You begin to feel not only embarrassment but also shame and self-hatred. "Why can't I do anything right?" you ask. And back and forth it goes, with Critical Parent dumping shame on Wounded Child, who feels worse and worse.

TA teaches us how to get out of this internal argumentation. We know that the Wounded Child has no ability to resist the Critical Parent, so we must depend on the Adult to do so. If our rational

Adult consciousness is ignorant and uninterested, however, Critical Parent will continue the abuse. An enlightened rational Adult can enter the dialogue with Critical Parent, as demonstrated below:

Critical Parent: "You blew it again! How many times have I told you that you just can't cook? Why did you have to pick such a hard recipe anyway? You can't do anything right!"

Wounded Child: Begins to feel anger toward herself.

Enlightened Adult: "Wait a minute now! I do too know how to cook! I do too know how to do lots of things right! I'm not a bad person; I only messed up this recipe, and I'll apologize to my company and send out for pizza."

Natural Parent: "You're only human. Everyone makes mistakes. You're still okay when you make mistakes."

Result: Natural Child feels accepted and validated within.

Only by engaging in this kind of internal self-talk can the Critical Parent be corrected and the Inner Wounded Child healed. The important task, then, is to empower the growth and development of one's Enlightened Adult state. This is where reading, reflection, study, workshops, lectures, the feedback of others, and other learning situations can help.

It is good news that you can so empower the growth of the Enlightened Adult, even though you are still struggling with Critical Parent and Wounded Child issues. The Enlightened Adult state enables you to break out of old patterns to take charge of your own life. In time the old Critical Parent tapes fade away, the Wounded Child is healed, and you live primarily out of the Enlightened Adult level, energized by the magical, mystical Natural Child within.

Steps to Retraining

For those seeking a way to relate this chapter's discussion of growth stages, habilitation, and transactional analysis to the Twelve Steps, I suggest that Steps Six and Seven can be used as steps of retraining.

Step Six

We're entirely ready to have God remove all these defects of character.

The term *defects of character* refers primarily to those distorted attitudes that lead us to feel shame, fear, and resentment. These are the three most harmful emotions. For addicts, these are the emotions that are medicated or numbed through use of the addictive mood-altering fix. When experiencing these emotions, addicts are strongly tempted to use their "fix of choice" to relieve this pain. For codependents, this fix is obsessing on another person's life and trying to control the other in some way.

It follows, then, that those who wish to be free from the slavery of addiction need to become free from emotional pain also. This requires changing those attitudes and behaviors that lead one to experience emotional pain. That is what Step Six is about.

Listed below are common defects of character that codependents and other addicts must struggle with.

- *Desire for control.* Wanting to control things that cannot be controlled.
- *Dishonesty.* Being untruthful in word and deed and — above all — about one's motives.
- *Willfulness.* Wanting to do things "my way."
- *Perfectionism.* Being impatient with mistakes made by oneself and others.
- *Procrastination.* Not finishing tasks on time.
- *Irresponsibility.* Not keeping one's commitments.
- *Vindictiveness.* Wanting to get back at others.
- *Self-pity.* Having a "poor me" attitude.
- *Self-righteousness.* Consistently thinking, "I am right and everyone else is wrong."
- *Low self-esteem.* Not liking oneself.
- *Grandiosity.* Exaggerating one's assets to impress others. Boasting.

- *Lust.* Engaging in sex without love and commitment.
- *Envy.* Wanting what others have.
- *Jealousy.* Feeling anger toward others for what they possess.
- *Avariciousness.* Being greedy and materialistic.

These and other defects of character can be found not only in addicts but also in all human beings who are spiritually immature. For addicts, however, these defects of character actually contribute to the addictive system of consciousness by causing emotional pain and defensiveness.

Most of these defects of character inhere from the dysfunctional inner dialogue between Critical Parent and Not-OK Child. For example, Critical Parent says, "It's not okay to make mistakes." Inner Child feels angry and defensive when mistakes are made. Critical Parent says, "People who have nicer things than you must be better people." Inner Child feels envious and jealous around prosperous people. Critical Parent says, "You're just dumb and stupid." Inner Child feels inadequate and has low self-esteem.

Two circumstances are necessary in working Step Six. The first is recognition of the nature of your defects of character. Listed below are three questions to ask yourself.

1. Which of the above defects of character do you identify with?
2. How do these defects of character show up in your daily experiences?
3. What kinds of consequences are you and others paying because of these defects of character?

By asking yourself these questions, you awaken a part of your consciousness that is not trapped in the addictive system. The "you" that "sees" these defects of character is not the addicted you but the True Self. Simply to practice self-honesty is a healing discipline.

The second essential for working Step Six is a willingness to be rid of these defects of character. This is more difficult than it sounds, for you can become so accustomed to experiencing yourself a certain way that you come to believe you cannot change. Furthermore, every one of these defects of character comes with a payoff of some kind. For example, procrastinators never have to have their work evaluated; self-righteous people feel morally superior; self-pitying people blame life for their problems and so avoid responsibility for changing. Giving up a defect of character means giving up the payoffs it brings with it. Generally, people are not willing to do this unless the harmful consequences of the defect exceed the payoffs.

If you feel ambivalent about giving up defects of character, be advised that they never go away on their own. They only get worse; and if you are an addict, they will lead to relapse. On the plus side, the serenity that comes when you have made progress in eliminating defects of character exceeds the payoffs these defects bring. This serenity cannot be described, however. It must be experienced.

Step Seven

Humbly asked Him to remove our shortcomings.

Step Seven recognizes that removing defects of character is not something that can be done by will power alone. We are as powerless over the tyranny of Critical Parent and Not-OK Inner Child as we are over our addictive fix.

Let us assume that you have worked Step Six, recognized your defects of character, and are willing to have them removed. What is required next is a surrender of these defects to the care of God. In recovery you are not remaking yourself but are allowing God to remake you into the person you were created to be. This surrender can come in prayer, where you offer yourself to God and ask for the grace to overcome the specific defect of character. You simply "turn it over," acknowledging your powerlessness to control yourself completely in this area. In addition you can allow yourself to desire freedom from this defect.

Of course, prayer is not all that you must do to be free; you must also use your will to cooperate with God's grace. If, for example, you are struggling with lust and have turned this over to God in prayer, then you must also avoid pornographic materials. And you must strive to check your lustful fantasies. If you do this, your mind will eventually yield. If you do not, then God's grace will be of little avail.

Summary

There are few adults who do not carry some emotional scars from childhood. The inadequacies in our developmental environment have left most of us suffering from the shaming influences of an internal Critical Parent and a Not-OK Inner Child. This is especially true for those who grew up in homes where a parent was an addict of some kind. These early-onset codependents suffer not only from their own addictions but also from the pains inflicted in their developmental environments. They feel inadequate, flawed, confused about identity, afraid of being abandoned, and anxious about getting close to others. In turn they "infect" their own children, spouses, and friends with their emotional "dis-eases."

There is a way out, but it requires taking responsibility for your own growth. This means empowering the rational Adult level of consciousness to challenge the oppressive rule of the Critical Parent. This Adult level must be educated, however, for it will become the means by which a new internal Nurturing Parent will eventually shape your emotional development.

Steps Six and Seven of the Twelve Steps teach us that eliminating defects of character is essential to recovery from addiction. They also point out the importance of spiritual centeredness for changing dysfunctional attitudes and behaviors. It is out of this spiritual centeredness that the Enlightened Adult, Nurturing Parent, and Natural Child begin to develop, bringing a new sense of joy and serenity in living.

For the Christian in recovery, much of what has been discussed in this chapter pertains to what Scripture describes as sin "in the flesh." The defects of character produced by the violent interaction between Critical Parent and Not-OK Inner Child lead addicts to act in many nonloving ways. Nonloving attitudes within lead to nonloving behaviors. This dynamic of nonlove is what we mean by sin. We are "infected" by this sin-disease from birth through the nonloving elements in our developmental environment.

Freedom from sin-disease begins when we recognize its existence and become entirely ready to be free of it (Step Six). The next step (Step Seven) is to identify ourselves with Christ, who has power over sin and who is the source of our True Self. This identification with Christ becomes incarnated in the individual through the struggle to avoid sin and to live a life of love.

CHAPTER FIVE
Resolving Emotional Pain

An important contribution to human understanding from the field of addiction counseling was identification of the "dry-drunk syndrome." Addiction counselors had long recognized that while many alcoholics could succeed in maintaining abstinence for a time, they were usually cranky, demanding, and moody during these periods. Although "dry," they still acted as if they were "drunk," hence the term, "dry drunk."

Family members frequently report that a dry drunk is as difficult to live with as a "wet drunk." After all, it is not the drinking and drugging that bothers family members but the abusive, unpredictable behavior that comes with it. A dry drunk is a persistence of abusive, unpredictable behavior in abstinence.

Through the years we have come to recognize the dry-drunk syndrome in a variety of other addictions besides alcoholism. Gamblers, too, begin to get edgy without their fix; so do sex addicts, work addicts, and codependents. After a few days away from the person with whom they are obsessed, many codependents begin to feel lonely, cranky, and lost.

Far from negating the importance of abstinence, the dry-drunk syndrome teaches us that addicts need more than abstinence from a fix if they are to enjoy life. The addict must recenter his or her life in God and learn healthy ways to meet needs. This recentering and retraining leads to better health by diminishing the amount of emotional pain produced by the psyche. An issue that remains, however, is what to do about the emotional pain one already carries. This pain, it turns out, is the cause of dry-drunk behavior.

Addiction and Emotional Pain

The capacity to feel is part of our basic human nature. Feelings are the primary self-experience of the child and continue to play a vital role throughout adulthood. The purpose of feelings is to teach us the meaning of the events taking place in our lives. In general, painful feelings teach us that something is wrong — usually with the way we perceive reality. Pleasant feelings teach us that we are meeting our needs in a healthy way. To be in touch with our feelings, then, is to be in touch with our inner sense of the meaning of life. An awareness of this sense of meaning is important to our spiritual awareness.

A problem develops, however, when we use addictive fixes to change our moods. Addictive fixes such as mood-altering chemicals, sexual activity, and even sweets direct our attention away from pain and toward pleasure or euphoria. They do this by directly stimulating the pleasure centers of the brain or by shifting our attention to something else, perhaps obsessing on another person, winning at the gambling table, working, and so on. These addictive fixes "trick" the body by giving us good feelings for doing something that is bad for us — which goes against the usual course of nature. This tricking of the body is part of the physiological dimension of addiction.

What happens to the emotional pain within when we use addictive fixes to escape? Some of this pain does get expressed during the fix-episode, as when a drunk person cries about a lost relationship. Even so, these feelings are drug-affected, so the issues that lie behind them are not resolved. However, most emotional pain is simply forgotten during a fix-episode, thus contributing to the emotional dimension of addiction. Unresolved emotional pain does not go away; it merely passes out of consciousness for a while.

Consider the plight of Sam. Sam has a toothache. Toothaches hurt, so Sam naturally realizes that something is wrong with his tooth. As an intelligent, conscious human being, he also knows that the dentist's office is the most logical place to get lasting relief from this pain. Sam's intelligent consciousness also knows that trips to the dentist are often painful, however, so he decides to take the pain pill left over from an operation a few months earlier. The pain pill brings relief from the toothache. It also makes Sam feel lightheaded — *high!* After a few hours the pill wears off, and his toothache is back again, only worse now, for the degeneration of the tooth is more advanced. Sam takes another pain pill to make it through the night. The addictive cycle has begun.

People use addictive fixes to escape from many "emotional toothaches." All human beings experience grief, hurt, disappointment, resentment, shame, and fear at some time. If we are open to feeling these pains and talking them through with a compassionate listener, we can learn from them and grow. This learning and growing is what resolving emotional pain is all about. When emotional pain is not resolved, it remains inside us — usually in the bodily tissues where we experience it as stress. If the body becomes very stressed, this negative energy causes migraine headaches, muscular aches, lower back pain, ulcers, and high blood pressure. Furthermore, negative emotional energy lowers the responses of the immune system, making us more vulnerable to diseases. We pay a high price for living in emotional pain.

In addition to hurting the body, unexpressed emotional pain contributes to a deterioration of the personality. Addicts are often negative, defensive, grandiose, and condescending. Minor hurts in the present moment resonate with their inner pain, building molehills to mountainous status. Frequently, this pain is projected onto others who are then viewed as threats to the addict's security.

Thus do addicts react inappropriately toward others, contributing to deeper loneliness within.

The dry drunk, then, is a person who, after giving up the addictive fix, still suffers from emotional pain. Without the addictive fix to give relief, the dry drunk "acts out" these emotions — frequently in antisocial ways. This only causes more emotional pain, however, leading the dry drunk to crave relief from the pain within.

Freedom from emotional pain is a necessary part of recovery. Addictive fixes look more tempting when one is in emotional pain. That is why Steps Four, Five, Eight, and Nine of the Twelve Steps are so important to recovery from all addictions, including codependency. If the addict works these steps, emotional pain can be resolved. If she or he does not work these steps, dry-drunk behavior will result. And efforts toward re-centering and retraining will be seriously hampered.

Cleansing the Soul

Perhaps the most serious consequence of codependency and other addictions is the loss of the capacity for self-honesty. We become deluded — sincerely deluded — about our motives and behavior. We rationalize and justify our behavior under the pretense of noble motives, all the while pursuing the fix to avoid emotional pain. This delusion is such that we are not even aware that it is going on; it happens automatically. "The disease thinks for you," as it is sometimes expressed. Discerning the difference between delusional thinking and honest thinking is one of the major tasks in recovery.

If you have begun with the work outlined in the previous pages, you are in a good position now to explore deeply the roots of your own delusional thinking. Step One helped you to see how the fix didn't really work; Steps Two and Three helped you to re-center your life in your Higher Power; Steps Six and Seven helped to empower the ascendance of your enlightened rational Ego. This preliminary work is important, for it is this Adult Ego centered in the Higher Power that will be doing the inventory called for in Step Four. Without this preliminary work, inventory can become a work of the Critical Parent and hence a traumatic experience for the Inner Child.

Step Four

Made a searching and fearless moral inventory of ourselves.
Do you really know what makes you tick?

Most people don't. They are aware of what they want others to believe about what makes them tick, but they are deluded about their own inner motives. As noted previously, this dishonesty about motives is especially true of codependents and other addicts.

Step Four brings a return to the dynamic of recognition characteristic of Step One. Step Four is about seeing yourself through the lenses of honesty. This seeing further dissolves the roots of addiction by bringing them to consciousness. What conscious Adult Ego does not see remains in the unconscious, and that which is unconscious has power over consciousness. Seeing, then, is about naming your innermost thoughts, feelings, and motives. This dynamic is similar in many ways to the process of exorcism, in which the troublesome demons must be named — or brought to consciousness — before they can be dismissed in the name of God.

Many resources are available to assist you in doing Step Four. My book *Becoming a New Person: Twelve Steps to Christian Growth* (Liguori Publications, 1984) includes a long list of questions to help you explore your strengths and weaknesses. AA, Al-Anon, and ACOA, as well as the many excellent books currently available on addiction and recovery, are also helpful sources for working Step Four. Some inventory guides focus on the Ten Commandments, the seven deadly sins, and other traditional guides to reflection. Others use psychosocial categories. If you are not sure how to do an inventory, these guides can be helpful.

Two additional points need to be made about Step Four. The first is that this inventory should focus on your morality. It is to be a "searching and fearless *moral* inventory" and not an inventory of your self-concept. This means that you should focus on your values — what you believe are the best ways for you to go about meeting your needs. You also need to examine how your behavior has conflicted with your values. Finally, note how you have been true to your values.

When you act contrary to your values, you experience guilt. Because all addicts act contrary to their values, all addicts suffer from guilt. Many go a step further, allowing Critical Parent to judge them as bad people, which results in inner shame. Addicts are defensive about their guilt and shame, but this defensiveness fails to bring relief from pain. On the contrary, the defensive addict is moved to use the fix to escape the pain.

Second, and equally important, this inventory is to be undertaken in a completely nonjudgmental state of mind. This is only possible for the Enlightened Adult Ego, which you are more in touch with by now. If you get in touch with painful feelings, allow yourself to experience them without judging yourself as a good or bad person on the basis of your feelings. To do this, you will need to involve your Nurturing Parent attitude in the inventory.

Take your time. Do not rush through the inventory. Be as honest as you can, realizing that you will not know everything about your inner life even after doing the inventory. God allows us to work with only a little at a time, so you will need to repeat this inventory in the future — every year or so.

Step Five

Admitted to God, to ourselves, and to another human being the exact nature of our wrongs.

No house is clean until the dirt is eliminated. The inventory you did in Step Four put you in touch with the dirt. Step Five gets rid of it.

Most people struggle with the part of Step Five that requires telling another human being "the exact nature of our wrongs." It is hard enough to admit the nature of your wrongs to God and yourself. However, God, after all, is forgiving, and you had a pretty good idea of what was there anyway. Isn't the forgiveness of God and self enough?

To answer this question, you must first recognize that human beings are not just individuals but members of a larger community. Your individual life impacts the lives of other individuals, just as their lives affect you. When you sin — or contract yourself away from others in nonloving behaviors and attitudes — you deprive the community of your gifts and energies. Even if your behavior is not overtly abusive, the nonloving self-concentration of isolation and noninvolvement has consequences for the community. Just think what would happen if several of your lung cells decided they simply would not work anymore. Your whole body would suffer in some manner. So it is with the individual and the community.

Step Five invites you to reconnect with the community by sharing deeply of yourself with another human being. The role of this person, who can be a minister or a sponsor from a Twelve Step group (but should not be your spouse), is to function as a non-judgmental listening and validating presence — sort of an external Nurturing Parent.

Having listened to hundreds of Fifth Steps myself, I can testify that it is a truly humbling experience for both the sharer and the listener. A sort of miracle takes place, too, in that shortly after leaving the session, I forget what was discussed. Other Fifth Step listeners have reported the same experience. The sense of unburdening and forgiveness realized by the person sharing is enjoyed by the listener as well. It is a grace-filled experience, a true welcoming back to the human community.

As a Roman Catholic, I see in Steps Four and Five something of what the sacrament of reconciliation is meant to be. In this sacrament we have an opportunity to cleanse our souls of guilt, shame, resentment, jealousy, and other poisons. By sharing this inventory with a priest, we receive in return the reassurance of God's forgiveness and the forgiveness of the community whom we have cheated through our sinful self-contraction.

Making Amends

During the years I worked as a family therapist with a chemical-dependency treatment center, patients and their families frequently complained when we asked them to talk about painful issues from the past with one another. "Can't we let bygones be bygones?" they would ask. "The past is past. What matters now is the future."

Of course, the future matters, but so does the present and the past. And we know for certain that unresolved emotional issues from the past will surely contaminate the present and become projected into the future.

Steps Four and Five help us begin resolving emotional issues. Nevertheless, the founders of AA discovered that if we are to be truly free, we must go even further and make amends to those we have harmed. If we fail to make amends, the unresolved emotional pain that remains between us and those we have harmed will prevent us from experiencing serenity. We are uncomfortable in the presence of these others, for there is always guilt, shame, envy, or resentment lurking in the background. Therefore, we must work Steps Eight and Nine to be truly free.

Steps Eight and Nine

Made a list of all persons we had harmed, and became willing to make amends to them all and *Made direct amends to such people wherever possible, except when to do so would injure them or others.*

These two steps are practically self-explanatory. You do exactly what Step Eight says: Make a list of people who have been affected by your behavior. In a second column, write down the issues and incidents that have come between you and each of these people. In a third column, write down how these issues and incidents have affected your relationship with each person. Finally, to complete Step Eight, write in a fourth column how you can make amends to these people. Complete willingness to make amends is a requirement of this step.

I am firmly convinced of the value of this written list. In doing family therapy, my co-therapist and I asked family members and patients to make such lists to share openly in the group. Many times family members complained that they did not need to make a list because they had it all in their heads. When it was their turn to share, however, they rambled on in generalities and were not able to gain any relief.

On the other hand, those who made written lists shared that the process helped jog their memories, allowing repressed feelings to rise to the surface. While this caused initial discomfort, the long-term effect of facing these feelings and sharing them appropriately was relief. The lists helped patients and family members see clearly what had happened in their relationships. They also helped them to be specific in talking about their issues.

Of course, most people who work Steps Eight and Nine will not be doing so in family therapy. The usual format for making amends is letters, phone calls, and personal visits. Sometimes you may choose to let an old issue drop if the effort to make amends would injure you or others more than it would help. This is especially true concerning adulterous affairs about which your spouse may be ignorant. Surely the affair affected your relationship, but to share it now may bring more hurt than cure. Step Nine reminds us that there is a virtue greater than honesty, and it is charity.

The Twelve Steps, originally written to help alcoholics in recovery, are most helpful for codependents and other addicts as well. However, a problem often arises with Steps Eight and Nine, which focus entirely on the wrongs the addict has done to others and not on wrongs suffered by the addict. This emphasis is appropriate for alcoholics, especially those who have been verbally and/or physically abusive. But even such abusive alcoholics have been hurt by others too, and this pain causes defensiveness in relationships.

Codependents and ACOA's are probably more in touch with how they have been hurt than how they have hurt others. Therefore, to make true amends in a relationship, it is helpful to make a second Step Eight list — one of how others have hurt you and how this has affected your relationship with them. Making this list may be even more painful than the first — especially for ACOA's.

Working Step Nine toward those who have hurt you requires discernment. The most effective approach is to share how the other person's specific behaviors affected you emotionally, financially, physically, and spiritually. Avoid being judgmental and critical and stick to the discussion of issues and behaviors and their consequences to you. Letters, phone calls, and personal meetings are each appropriate in their place. The most desirable outcome of this sharing would be an apology from the other. Even if an apology is not forthcoming, however, it is important to go through the process for yourself.

Of course, the proviso in Step Nine about avoiding unnecessary pain needs to be considered here too. Sometimes the people who have hurt you will hurt you again if you share your pain with them. If you suspect that could happen, you might decide to write a letter and then burn it (perhaps after reading it to a minister or a sponsor in the program). Say a prayer for the person who hurt you as the letter burns. This will help you let go of hurt and resentment.

In a gospel corollary to Steps Eight and Nine, Jesus said: "If you bring your gift to the altar, and there recall that your brother has anything against you, leave your gift there at the altar, go first and be reconciled with your brother, and then come and offer your gift" (Matthew 5:23-24). The guilt, shame, envy, jealousy, hurt, and resentments in our human relationships impede our spiritual growth. Jesus is telling us that if we are to get straight with God, we must also get straight with our fellow human beings.

We should, however, give ourselves time to make amends with others. Many times people in recovery want to be straight about everything "yesterday." This is impatience and perfectionism now brought into the recovery program. It takes most people years of living in addiction before they get into recovery; making amends may also take years. Forgiveness is not an all-or-nothing experience but something that happens by degrees. All that is necessary is the willingness to forgive and be forgiven and to make the effort to work Steps Eight and Nine.

Staying Clean and Sober

Steps Four, Five, Eight, and Nine bring a real housecleaning. Keeping the house clean is another matter, however. That's where Step Ten comes in.

Step Ten

Continued to take personal inventory and when we were wrong promptly admitted it.

Step Ten is the relapse-prevention step. It includes the dynamics of inventory (Step Four) and admission (Steps Five, Eight, and Nine). Most people work this step daily by pausing at the end of the day to reflect on what has happened. In working it yourself, you might ask yourself the following questions.

- What happened today?
- Was I honest?
- Was I charitable?
- Was I selfish and controlling?
- Do I need to make amends to anyone?

Some people write their reflections in a journal. I like to take a walk and think about them.

By working Step Ten, you continue to cultivate the "seeing-awareness" so essential for maintaining responsibility for your life. If you do not cultivate awareness, you will become more unconscious and prone to moods and compulsions. With unconscious living will come addiction, and you want to be done with that! The best antidote to relapse, then, is awareness. And awareness is what Step Ten calls for.

Another fruit of working Step Ten is that small problems are prevented from growing into large problems. When your mistakes are noted and corrected daily, they do not have time to compound themselves through the weeks and months. Your life becomes simpler. As a result of working the Twelve Steps, you will discover one day that you no longer have to deal with contaminating influences of the past. You can concentrate on the problems of each day. In life we are never through with daily problems, but they are a lot more manageable if they are just that: daily problems and not problems from the past. To keep daily problems from growing, however, you will need to work Step Ten.

In the Catholic tradition, the corollary to Step Ten can be found in the Examen of Conscience that Saint Ignatius of Loyola formulated as a daily discipline for his Jesuits. Saint Ignatius is said to have considered this discipline to be more valuable than daily prayer, although he surely did not mean it to replace daily prayer.

To benefit fully from Step Ten, you must follow up on the insights you gain from your daily reflection. If, for example, you discover that you have not been completely honest with another person, you must do what is necessary in the spirit of Step Nine to get straight with him or her. If you discover that you have behaved rudely or selfishly toward someone, you must go and apologize to that person.

Obviously, Step Ten is a difficult discipline, especially at first. Taking a look at yourself is not always fun; you might not like what you see. Be gentle in this looking, however, remembering that God has already forgiven you everything. You're working the step to grow; that is what is important. By working this step daily, you will become aware of the many ways in which you are, in fact, making progress. As they say in Twelve Step programs, it is this progress — not perfection — that is important.

CHAPTER SIX

What Is Christian Love?

In *The Essentials of Chemical Dependency,* Robert and Mary McAuliffe define chemical dependency as "a sick or pathological relationship of a person to a mood-altering chemical in expectation of a rewarding experience." Substance-abuse counselors sometimes apply this same formula to codependency, defining it as "a sick or pathological relationship of a person to another person in expectation of a rewarding experience."

Codependency, then, is a sick love relationship. Recovery is about learning to love in a healthy manner. In one sense codependents have it harder than chemically dependent people. You can live without mood-altering chemicals, but you cannot live without love. Recovering codependents must learn to love without enabling and controlling, and this is not easy.

Codependents must struggle with the question of what, precisely, it means to love another person. What is the difference between healthy love and sick love? It is here that the example of Jesus of Nazareth can help us.

Christianity has much to say about love. In fact, the essence of our religion is love. As 1 John 4:16 puts it, "We have come to know and to believe in the love God has for us. God is love, and whoever remains in love remains in God and God in him." Jesus teaches that love of God, neighbor, and self fulfills the law and the prophets. (See Matthew 7:12.) In an ideal world, the Church would be a community in which recovering codependents could learn about healthy love.

Unfortunately, this is not always the case. One of the saddest things I have seen through the years is the disappointment many recovering codependents find in the Church. Some have gone so far as to tell me that the Church actually teaches codependency. In *Co-Dependence: Misunderstood-Mistreated,* Anne Wilson Schaef writes, "The dishonesty in the church is perhaps the most devastating institutionalization of dishonesty in our society, because it takes place within the realm of the spirit — the very essence of our being. The church teaches so many forms of dishonesty that I find it difficult to know where to start." She then goes on to give examples of narrow-minded teachings concerning God and relationships.

While I agree with Schaef and others that many distortions about love are propounded from Christian pulpits and classrooms, I maintain that the *true* Christian teachings about love lead to healthy relationships. This chapter will explore the differences between sick love, or codependency, and healthy Christian love.

What Christian Love Is Not

In reflecting on the meaning of Christian love, it will be helpful to consider some common distortions about love. If these distortions become part of one's Critical Parent system, they can lead to codependent behaviors.

First, Christian love is not codependency. Christian love does not call for a giving of yourself that enables another to act irresponsibly. Neither does Christian love call for a "laying down one's life for one's friends" that results in a negation of your giftedness and uniqueness.

Certain teachings commonly heard in Christian circles, however, can lead to enabling and unhealthy giving of self in practice.

Some of these teachings are listed below.

- *I am my neighbor's keeper.* The codependent interprets this as meaning that we are responsible for one another's feelings and happiness. A healthy understanding is that we are all interdependent and have the responsibility to help victims of injustice.
- *Love equals good works.* The distortion is that only those who do good works can be said to be loving. If, in addition, we define what those good works would be, then we would judge people according to whether or not they're doing those works. Of course, it is possible to do good works and be empty or resentful inside. That is a further distortion of this Christian motto.
- *Love means putting others before self.* This teaching, taken literally, will produce codependency. At times self-denial is appropriate behavior. Parents waking in the night to care for a hungry baby must suspend their own need for sleep for the sake of the baby. The problem comes when we use self-denial as an absolute indicator of love, never getting around to our own needs. Even if other people's needs are not as important as our own, we set aside our own needs to meet theirs. Such self-denying behavior distorts true Christian love.
- *It is better to give than to receive.* As with the self-denying distortion of Christian love described above, codependents interpret "giving" as putting others first. They regard receiving as selfish. Actually, for codependents, staying on the giving side is a way to be in control and avoid feeling vulnerable.
- *Love means I must never say no to someone in need.* A literal interpretation of this teaching would result in the loss of boundaries that characterizes codependency. Sometimes you must say no, even to those in need. If you respond to every request for charity that comes your way through television, radio, and the mail, you will go broke. The true Christian value is to remain open in your heart while giving what you can.

- *It is better to work than to play.* ACOA's have trouble with this one. Many ACOA's not only suffer the codependent consequence of loss of self but also lose their Inner Child. They grew up too quickly and missed their childhood. Their parents discouraged child-play and forced them to become too responsible too young. As adults, they still feel guilty when they are not doing something productive. This attitude distorts the Christian value of productive labor.

- *We should never judge others.* Codependents distort the Christian warning about judging others to mean we should not even confront unhealthy behavior. Codependents make no distinction between person and behavior; to confront someone's behavior is to say that the person is bad. They neglect to challenge harmful and inappropriate behavior, further enabling irresponsibility.

- *We should be perfect as God is perfect.* ACOA's and codependents understand this teaching to mean we should not make mistakes. Because codependency is rooted in the experience of conditional love, the attempt to be perfect is an effort to obtain love through perfect works. It is not a sin to make mistakes; it is human to make mistakes. Sin is a *willful* neglect of what is good, or a *willful* consent to do what is bad. Often our mistakes concern not willfulness or being good and bad but merely human weaknesses and limitations. It is harmful to judge yourself as bad because you make mistakes. The perfection Jesus asks for is that we do our best, then leave the rest in God's hands.

- *Do not be angry.* Codependents interpret this teaching of Christ to mean feeling angry is wrong, bad, and sinful. Codependents are angry and resentful on the inside. Since they believe it is bad to be angry, they repress these feelings and try hard to be "nice." This facade of niceness keeps codependents out of touch with their anger. Anger is a feeling, and feelings are neither bad nor good. It is what we do with our feelings that is bad or good. Jesus is talking about harboring resentment and vindictiveness. These are choices about how to deal with anger — bad choices!

- *We should not expect happiness in this life.* I have heard this said in therapy groups by codependents who had resigned themselves to being trapped for the rest of their earthly days in an unhealthy relationship. The truth is that we can begin to experience something of heaven even in this life. Distorted beliefs such as this are really about being a victim and martyr.
- *To forgive means to forget.* We discussed the difference between forgiving and forgetting in the previous chapter. While you may never forget what has happened, you can let go of resentment, a kind of emotional forgetting.

All these teachings give a distorted picture of the meaning of Christian love. Each of them contains a kernel of truth, but taken out of context, they lose their force. When taught by codependents who are active in ministry, they become one of the means by which the Church contributes to the spread of codependency.

What Is Love?

The word *love* is used in many contexts. We speak of loving ice cream, being in love with another person, needing to feel loved, and so forth. Many languages use different words to describe different types of love. In English, however, we use the same word, love, to describe different experiences. This undoubtedly contributes to some confusion. For example, it is common to find people projecting the love their parents had for them onto God — as though God were some kind of Super-Parent.

True, the Scriptures use examples of human love experiences to tell us something about God. Jesus calls God his Father, and the author of the Song of Songs speaks of God as a lover. If a person's human father was abusive, which was often true for ACOA's, he or she will not find the image of God the Father attractive. God-as-lover is not attractive to codependents trying to escape addiction to distorted romantic love. The language of the Twelve Steps, which speaks of God as a Higher Power, is often helpful to codependents and ACOA's for this reason.

While the Twelve Steps outline a powerful spiritual growth process, they nevertheless leave open questions about the nature of God. Anyone practicing the Steps must eventually come to terms with his or her own beliefs about God. Of course, there is a difference between a spiritual program and a religious commitment. The participant is free to use the spiritual program of the Twelve Steps as a way to deepen his or her religious commitment.

What we believe about God is important, for these beliefs color our views of self, others, relationships, the world, and the meaning of life. Unfortunately, many people in recovery have rejected Christianity on the basis of their poor human relationships. Actually, they have not rejected Christianity but the distortions of Christianity and of God presented to them by their families and, often, by their churches. Often these people go on to profess faith in a God who loves them unconditionally — which is exactly what Christianity teaches. What they miss, however, is the joy of worshiping this God in a community. Twelve Step groups are not a substitute for membership in a church.

In reflecting on the meaning of Christian love, we must say from the outset that Scripture equates the nature of God with love. As Scripture puts it, "God is love," and love is as mysterious and beyond definition as God. The statements about love discussed in the previous section are distortions precisely because they try to limit love to certain actions, and this cannot be done.

The Nature of Christian Love

While we may be unable to define love or pin it down, this does not mean that we are ignorant of its ways. Jesus of Nazareth shows us, in human form, how love thinks and acts. He reveals the inner nature of God. By reading in Scripture about his life, we come to a better understanding of the meaning of love. The best way to learn to love is to follow the example of Christ.

In reflecting on the life of Christ, we learn several important lessons about love. The first is that God's love is unconditional; there is nothing we can do to earn God's love. The terms for our relationship with God are not like those in dysfunctional families. We do not have to do good works and act perfectly to earn God's approval. God loves us exactly as we are because *God is love.* God can do nothing but love because that is who God is. The realization that God already loves us regardless of what we do is the key to entering eternal life. There is nowhere to go and nothing to do to earn this love.

What about sin? Does God love us even when we sin?

These questions are answered clearly in Christ's teaching and life. Yes, God loves us even when we sin. There is not one example in Scripture of Christ turning away from someone because that person was too bad for him. In fact, it was precisely his willingness to be available to sinners that scandalized the Jewish leaders. So we can have no doubt about it: God loves sinners, and this means you!

Unlike dysfunctional people, however, Christ made a distinction between person and behavior. He loved people, but he frequently disagreed with and confronted unhealthy and sinful behavior. He did not judge people on the basis of behavior, but he did judge behavior on the basis of whether or not it was moral or immoral. "Love the sinner, but hate the sin" was his attitude.

God hates sin. God, who is love, created human beings to know and share in that love by helping to shape the creation. Therefore, we, created in God's image and likeness, are also love. When we sin, we act against our true nature. We distort what God has created, and we spread our evil and distortion to others by mistreating them. The consequences of our nonlove have even spread to creation, threatening the very basis of life on our planet. What we have done with the gift of life God has given us is equivalent to hoodlums throwing mud on the masterpiece of a painter. It destroys the masterpiece and insults the painter. We are magnificent beings acting like spoiled children, and this is an injustice toward God and one another. God still loves each of us but nonetheless hates all this nonloving selfish behavior.

This brings us to a critical point in our reflection on love. God has to put up with selfish creatures the same way codependents do. How does God handle it? Does God enable us or try to control us into shaping up?

The answer, of course, is that God continues to love us while allowing us to experience our consequences. God has given us the gift of himself in Christ and the gift of the Church to manifest the divine presence on earth. Beyond this, however, God does nothing, for to do more would violate our freedom, an essential condition for loving. As love, God allows us to use our freedom in destructive ways.

Many people have a problem with this reasoning. They believe that an all-powerful God should rescue us from the evil we have created through our own sick minds. They fail to realize that even if God did rescue us, we would create the same mess again in a short time out of the same sick minds. What God wants for us is not a short-term fix (which is what enabling brings) but a long-term cure. What God wants for us is conversion.

One way of pulling all this together is to realize that God has put us here to grow. Love is pro-growth. We need love to grow as plants need water and sunshine. We also need pruning; that is, we need to learn from the consequences of our behavior. Because God wants us to grow to become fully mature in Christ, God allows us to suffer. Enabling behavior is different in that it prevents people from growing and taking responsibility for their behavior by removing their suffering.

What about the death of Christ? We say that he died for our sins. Does this mean that he took responsibility for our behavior?

As these questions show, there is a codependent way of looking at the death of Christ. The difference is this: enablers do for others what they can and should do for themselves. It is not enabling to do for others what they cannot do for themselves.

The Redemption does for us what we could not do for ourselves — namely, enter the life of the Trinity. By taking on our nature and living our life, God, in Christ, has opened the way for the human race to experience the inner life of God. As any practicing Christian knows, faith does not leave one free from sin; the struggle with sin continues, and Christ does not take this away. Rather, he gives us his Spirit to overcome sin. Without his Spirit, we cannot live his life. Therefore, his incarnation, death, resurrection, ascension, and gift of the Spirit are gifts, not enablements.

Loving God's Will

From our reflection on the Scriptures, we come to realize that God is love, and that we, who are created in God's image and likeness, are called to lead a life of love. In our innermost nature we are completely one with God. When we act lovingly, we are simply exercising our True Self. When we are nonloving, we are exercising our false self.

By working Step Eleven, we come to embrace the call to live the life of Love.

Step Eleven

Sought through prayer and meditation to improve our conscious contact with God as we understood Him praying only for knowledge of His will for us and the power to carry that out.

If God is love and we are God's image and likeness, then prayer becomes the most authentic exercise of our humanity. In prayer we are seeking to awaken to our true self, the person we are in God.

This means that we must give time to be with God in prayer just as we must give time to stay connected in love with another person.

The first and most important commandment given to us by Christ is to "love the Lord your God with all your heart, with all your soul, with all your mind, and with all your strength" (Mark 12:30). If we are to be truly ourselves, we must love God above all else. All addictions will eventually fall away when we love God most. The best way to grow in the love of God is through prayer.

Mother Teresa wrote:

The fruit of silence is prayer.

The fruit of prayer is faith.

The fruit of faith is love.

The fruit of love is service.

Prayer comes before faith and love and service. People who attempt loving service without prayer often end up codependent.

Space does not permit an extensive discussion of the dynamics of prayer. As Mother Teresa's formula notes, silence is indispensable — especially in our noisy world. Spending time in silence, reading Scripture, visiting the Blessed Sacrament, being present to God in nature — these are all good ways to grow in prayer. Make a commitment to spend time with God daily and stick to this commitment come what may.

Step Eleven notes that we should pray for God's will and the power to carry it out. We know for sure that it is God's will that we grow in the fruits of the Spirit: "love, joy, peace, patience, kindness, generosity, faithfulness, gentleness, self-control" (Galatians 5:22-23). When you pray for these, your prayer will be answered quickly. God may not give you more money or a better house or good weather this weekend, but God does want you to grow in the Spirit. This is where happiness is to be found anyway; the rest is short-term thrills.

Reaching Out

The second great commandment given by Christ is that we should love our neighbor as ourselves. (See Mark 12:31.) He says this commandment is like the first. I take this to mean that the love we discover in prayer is the same love we discover in ourselves and in loving one another. It also means we cannot separate these two commandments, for they go together.

Step Twelve

Step Twelve captures the spirit of the second great commandment.

Having had a spiritual awakening as a result of these steps, we tried to carry this message to (alcoholics), and to practice these principles in all our affairs.

The first part of this step includes a promise that those who work Steps One through Eleven will have a spiritual awakening. They will know the love of God and will begin to awaken to the realization of their true selves.

The second part of this step encourages a sharing of this new life with others. A children's song says that love grows when you give it away. A popular adage advises that you can't give what you don't have, and you can't keep what you don't share. If you don't work the first eleven steps, you won't have much to give; but if you don't share what you've learned, you won't grow. Many implications are here for those in the helping professions such as counseling and ministry.

When we practice these principles in all our affairs, we become people of integrity. We lead lives of love and honesty, not because we might go to hell for neglecting these virtues, but because in practicing them we are being true to our real selves. To do otherwise would mean returning to the addictive state of consciousness we are striving to leave behind.

Summary

Codependency is a distortion of love. It is caring for people in an unhealthy way. The enabling of codependency allows people to become more irresponsible and leads to preoccupation and misery for the codependent.

Christian love, on the other hand, accepts people as they are while challenging them to grow. Because God does not enable our irresponsibility, we should not enable one another. Instead, we must learn to let people learn from their mistakes. We also need to learn when it is appropriate to help others and to confront their irresponsible behavior.

Learning to love in a healthy way is what recovery from codependency and other addictions is really about. Christianity has much to teach us about love. We learn that love cannot be reduced to simplistic mottoes and slogans because love is the very essence of the mysterious God. We learn, too, that Jesus Christ shows us how God loves.

When we love God above all else, our lives become properly focused. Earthly things take on their true perspective; we awaken to our true self in Christ. Step Eleven encourages us to cultivate this relationship with God through prayer, making God's will our true happiness.

Step Twelve brings it all together, validating the spiritual awakening that has taken place, while encouraging us simply to share what we have learned with others. This step also implies, however, that we must get our own house in order first if we are to be of much help to others. This is a most important lesson for codependents to learn.

CHAPTER SEVEN
Codependency and Ministry

An old saying goes, "If you want to belong to a perfect church, then look around and find one. But know that as soon as you join it, it shall no longer be a perfect church."

It should come as no surprise to anyone that the Church is not a perfect community. The media flaunted the recent sex scandals and financial abuses of televangelists and Catholic clergy for all to see. While many are scandalized by the faults of these and other professional ministers, most people realize that the Church is a community of human beings, all of whom have their weaknesses. To believe that the Church could be otherwise is to misunderstand the nature of the Church.

Of course, many people in both Catholic and Protestant denominations were taught to believe that priests and religious and other ministers were next to God in spiritual and moral status. Such people become easily scandalized when they discover that Father has a drinking problem or Sister has a male friend. They have made the unfortunate mistake of allowing the credibility of God and religion to rest for them on the actions of mere human beings. Because Church leaders know these are easily scandalized people, they try to deal with problems as discreetly as possible.

There is certainly no need to broadcast the problems of Church leaders from the rooftops. The Church, like most secular organizations, needs a process for helping troubled workers receive assistance. A problem arises, however, when discreet, responsible handling of a problem becomes full-blown denial and dishonesty. This often happens with regard to addicted Church leaders; entire communities can get caught up in enabling the dysfunctional behavior to escalate.

We must first get our own houses in order if we are to be of much help to others. This is as true for the Church as it is for the individual. If the Church is to be a model for the world to emulate, we must be a model worthy of emulation. We must practice justice within our communities, and we must deal appropriately with the problems that beset us. We must find ways to help addicted ministers, while examining the addictive processes within our communities.

Characteristics of Codependent Ministers

There are many codependent ministers in the Church. The symptoms of their disease are the same within ministry as within a troubled family, for it is the same disease manifesting itself in another context. It is precisely that context, however, that sometimes prevents us from recognizing codependent ministers. After all, ministry is about helping, serving, and giving — all of which codependents do in a distorted manner. How can we tell the difference between a hardworking minister and a codependent minister? Listed below are a few typical characteristics of codependent ministers.

- *Overresponsibility.* They feel personally responsible for things beyond their control, even to the point of feeling guilty and ashamed about some of these things.
- *Self-neglect.* They find it difficult to tend to their own needs and often feel guilty when they do so.
- *Unassertiveness.* They find it hard to say "no" to others and have a difficult time asking directly for their own needs to be met.

Instead, they use indirect methods of communication (games, insinuations, triangulation) to ask for their needs.

- *Inability to set boundaries.* They believe that every kind of good deed belongs to ministry and end up taking on more than they can do.
- *Nonconfrontiveness.* They feel guilty after pointing out unhealthy behavior in others, so they either avoid doing so or apologize profusely afterward.
- *Approval-seeking.* They do things that will put them in a good light with others, then make sure that others know about it.
- *People-pleasing.* They do things to please people to stay in the "good graces" of others. This is especially true in relationships with people who can bestow financial help.
- *Controlling.* They make themselves indispensable by becoming a "switchboard" to facilitate communication between groups. This is actually a way to secure their position and to control the information flow.
- *Rigidity.* They find it difficult to try something new, preferring instead to do things the way they have always been done.
- *Defensiveness.* They are not open to critical feedback about their own work and the projects they are involved in. This defensiveness sometimes extends to their religious community or denomination — "to criticize them is to criticize me" — an enmeshed situation.
- *Distorted teachings.* They teach the kinds of distortions about love, relationships, and service discussed in Chapter Six — for example, putting others first, the superiority of giving over receiving, and so on.
- *Comparing.* They evaluate their worth by measuring themselves against others. As a result, they feel superior to some and inferior to others.
- *Niceness.* They act nicely toward everyone and lose touch with their true feelings toward others.
- *Resentfulness.* Inside themselves, codependent ministers are

hurt, angry, and lonely. Because they do not resolve these feelings, they turn into resentments that often become channeled into idealistic causes or projected onto "oppressors."

- *Emotional numbness.* Because they repress or act out feelings, codependent ministers do not know what they feel. They frequently delude themselves about this numbness, saying that they are thinkers, not feelers, or that they are in a spiritual state of consciousness that transcends feeling.
- *Depression.* Because they feel compelled to be always nice to everyone, codependent ministers repress their emotional pain. This inevitably leads to psychological depression.
- *Loss of self.* After a while the codependent minister faces an identity crisis that may take expression in the spiritual realm ("where did the Lord go?"). They lose a sense of who they are, what their giftedness is, and how they are called to share their giftedness in the community.

Codependent ministers often become burned out. Much has been written about burnout in ministry in recent years, but I have seen nothing that relates burnout to codependency. My own sense is that people who are assertive and who know how to set boundaries for themselves do not burn out. Codependents do not do either of these.

The Christian community often enables codependent ministers by admiring their "selfless" devotion to certain causes. This admiration gives the codependent the payoff of approval that feeds into the disease. When the codependent finally burns out, however, the community is frequently baffled. Sometimes even the burnout is admired as an example of Christian selfless giving. This is sick!

Christian selfless giving does not burn out. True Christian loving is a sharing of God's love, which is inexhaustible. Those who learn how to tap into God's love do not burn out.

Unfortunately, codependent ministers teach and model a distortion of God's love to the community. The neighborly love they teach is about approval and control rather than freedom and generosity. Because they compulsively focus on others, they inadvertently place love of neighbor above love of God, negating the first great commandment of Christ. Because their spirituality is bankrupt, they cannot lead others to the wells of eternal life. Their teaching is, instead, from the wells of Critical Parent, filled with shoulds, musts, and oughts. They use the tactics of guilt and shame to motivate people to generosity. Of course, there can be no true generosity in such a context.

Codependency in ministry helps no one and hurts everyone! The minister gets sicker, spreading his or her disease to others. The codependent pastor, especially, actually becomes an obstacle to the overall growth and development of the community.

In discussing why so many codependents are found in ministry, Anne Wilson Schaef and Diane Fassel (*The Addictive Organization*) point to addicted leaders, behavior patterns learned in the family of origin, the nature of the ministerial environment, and certain addictive dynamics of institutions.

The Problem of the Addicted Leader

One way that ministers develop codependency is by working with a leader who is an addict. Because most religious organizations operate out of a hierarchical structure, the addicted leader can affect a staff and community dramatically.

Quite obviously, a common form of addiction found among ministerial leaders is chemical dependency. Statistically, ministers hold up more than their share of chemical dependency. The drinking, drugging, and pill usage of the leader cause many problems for the staff. A far greater problem, however, is the leader's defensiveness, moodiness, rigidity, and unpredictability in following through on commitments. Everyone "walks around on eggshells." Staff members naturally find themselves trying to avoid upsetting the leader, taking over responsibilities that the leader has neglected, and facilitating communication between the leader and the community (triangulation). These forms of enabling behavior move staff members into their own codependency.

Entire communities can become enablers of their addicted leaders. An article in the May/June 1990 issue of *Common Boundary* magazine discusses the problem of addicted leaders in American Buddhist groups. Followers of American Buddhist leader Chogyam Trungpa were frequently baffled by his undisciplined behavior, which directly violated Buddhist principles. "He openly slept with students. In Boulder [Colorado, his headquarters] he lectured brilliantly, yet was sometimes so drunk that he had to be carried off stage or held upright in his chair," writes Katy Butler, author of the article. Despite this overt addictive behavior, no one in the community intervened in the disease. Some students actually believed he was in a spiritual state that transcended ordinary human consciousness. "We bought the story that it was a way of putting 'earth' into his system so he could...relate to us. It never occurred to anyone I knew that he was possibly an alcoholic, since that was a disease that could only happen to an ordinary mortal. And many of us were ignorant — we thought of an alcoholic only as the classic bum in the street," said one student. Even as he lay in his bed dying of alcoholism at the age of forty-seven, few of his students could openly acknowledge what was happening.

Similar examples abound in the Christian community. The example of Trungpa is so outstanding because of the dynamic of codependency that resulted when an addicted leader's followers enabled him in his addiction. The same thing happens when the addicted leader is a Catholic bishop or a mother superior. The hierarchical structure of the leadership and the special status accorded the leader make it difficult to confront him or her. Frequently the leader uses authority to "punish" those who do break the no-talk rule (for example, firing them from the staff or sending them on assignments to far-off places).

Sometimes the addiction of the leader is codependency. The focus of this codependency might be gaining the approval of a higher leader, the community, or even the staff. Such codependent leaders create problems because of their indirect communication, lack of assertiveness, and lack of focus.

The movie *Mass Appeal,* starring Jack Lemon, demonstrated this point dramatically. Lemon played a Catholic pastor who for years had spent his energy trying to maintain the approval of his community. When an idealistic young seminarian arrived as an assistant, the pastor was forced to face the consequences of his codependency. He realized that all this people-pleasing behavior had cost him his identity and his faith. He no longer knew who he was or what he believed. He drank alcohol to numb his pain, becoming alcoholic as well as codependent. Moreover, the community suffered, too, because they never received from him a challenge to grow. Although this was a movie, it was a good example of what is happening in many places.

Chemical dependency and codependency are not the only addictions affecting leaders. Like anyone else, leaders may be addicted to work, gambling, sex, overeating, and watching television. The sex and money addictions of televangelists have been described in lurid detail in magazines, before juries, and on television talk shows. Pedophilia, another form of sexual addiction, has also been discovered among the clergy and publicized in the mass media. The consequences to these ministers, their victims, and the entire Church have been severe. Staff members, boards of directors, and other governing groups carried on a great deal of enabling to conceal and minimize the nature of these problems.

Regardless of their power and authority, addicted leaders can be helped. If the staff and community can recognize the problem, perhaps they can make a conscious decision to avoid enabling the irresponsible behavior of the leader. They can also quit making excuses for the leader and might even decide to seek professional help for intervening on the leader's problem. While the problem remains unresolved, however, anyone working with an addicted leader should attend Al-Anon or Co-Dependents Anonymous meetings — if for no other reason than to avoid becoming enmeshed in the leader's problems. If you find yourself in such a setting and discover that it is not possible to remain healthy while ministering with an addicted leader, seriously consider resigning from the situation. Neither you, the leader, nor the community will benefit from your progressing in codependency.

Addictive Patterns From Childhood

Many ministers, of course, were codependents before they became active in ministry and are simply continuing in this pattern of behavior. The most common example of this is codependent adult children from dysfunctional families who are sometimes drawn to ministry out of their roles as family Hero or Caretaker.

Heroes, you will recall, bring self-worth to the family through achievement. If Heroes also served as Caretakers of emotionally needy family members, they are readily disposed to seek their achievement in a helping profession of some kind. The connection between Hero/Caretakers and counselors has been noted many times in the literature on addiction and codependency. A profession such as counseling gives such people an opportunity to continue proving their worth as human beings by helping others. At a deeper level, they are also on a quest to understand themselves and to get help for their own families. Most counselors will acknowledge this deeper motive to come to terms with their own feelings of confusion and anxiety.

What is true of counselors (and also nurses, teachers, doctors, and other helpers) is also true of ministers. Ministry is an esteemed position in most communities. Families who produce ministers are typically viewed in a positive light by the community. Thus it is not uncommon to find alcoholic families producing a minister or two. In many of these families (especially a few decades ago), certain young people in the family were practically groomed from birth for the ministry. The unspoken assumption here is "we can't be all that bad if one or two of our kids give their lives to the Lord." This is a powerful myth — one that goes virtually unchallenged in society.

Family Hero/Caretakers who move into ministry out of compulsive dynamics will find there a role that allows them to exercise their codependency to the fullest. As ministers they are expected to be strong for others, to care for others, to give without receiving, and to know what God wants for others. I cannot think of a role more likely to enable codependency to progress. Even ministers who do not come out of dysfunctional families will develop some of the symptoms of codependency because of these expectations, as we shall see in our next section.

How common is the Hero/ministry connection? Although I know of no research that addresses this topic specifically, I have done a few informal surveys of my own. At a recent workshop I presented on codependency, I asked for a show of hands from all ministers present who were oldest children. More than fifty percent of the ninety ministers present raised their hands. I next asked for a show of hands from all who identified themselves as Heroes of their families of origin. Most of the oldest adult children kept their hands raised and an additional twenty percent of the group raised their hands. It is most common for oldest children to be Heroes, but frequently others may be Heroes too — especially in large families.

A priest friend who went through treatment for ACOA issues conducted his own informal survey. He reported to me that over half of the hundred or so priests in the treatment program came from alcoholic families in the small Catholic diocese where he grew up and now serves. Almost half of these ACOA priests had developed alcoholism themselves, but only a few were in recovery.

All of this is not to say that family Heroes who become ministers cannot be authentic in their vocation. Undoubtedly, one's choice of any vocation — ministry and otherwise — is always colored with mixed motives. Some of these motives may be related to our family roles, but some may be in response to a call from God. We must be open to examining these motives, however, lest we become trapped in a role and experience emotional burnout as a consequence of our compulsivity. This openness to integrating one's inner world is especially critical for ministers. Without it, codependency will destroy the inner life of the minister and affect the spiritual health of the entire community.

Ministers who discover that early-onset codependency is affecting their lives and the lives of others will find a wide variety of helps available to them. Most cities have treatment centers that provide both inpatient and outpatient programs for adult children of dysfunctional families. Many helpful books, videotapes, and audiotapes are also available.

Discovering that one is an early-onset codependent is no reason to leave the ministry. When a priest I knew went through an ACOA program and recognized how his family Hero role had strongly affected his choice of vocation, he left the priesthood. I believe his decision was too hasty. The decision to break a life commitment — even one made for the wrong reasons — is very serious indeed! In his principles for the discernment of spirits, Saint Ignatius encourages one to make every effort to live out these life commitments, knowing that God's grace will surely be available.

On the other hand, early-onset codependents who enter recovery will certainly find it necessary to change many of their old ministerial strategies. They will begin to set boundaries and priorities and to take better care of themselves. The community may have a difficult time with this at first, but in the long run the community will benefit more from healthy ministers than from unhealthy ones. An ACOA in recovery can also be an important source of encouragement to other ACOA's in the community.

The Addictive Ministry Environment

There is probably no more esteemed role in a community than that of minister. Ministers are, after all, the people who help us to drink from the Living Waters of the Spirit. Every human society has maintained a place of honor for its shamans, gurus, rabbis, priests, nuns, and other ministers. We need these people to help us grow spiritually.

Paradoxically, while the minister's role is a truly honorable one, the dark side is that many, many expectations come with this role. This combination of high esteem and heavy expectations creates a double bind which may become an addictive trap.

A priest friend recently left the ministry for a couple of years. "I did not know who 'Steve' was anymore," he told me. "I knew who 'Father Steve' was. And the scary thing was that I had enough work to be Father Steve twenty-four hours a day. But I wondered if somewhere along the line I didn't lose Steve too." Of course, he was talking about how easy it is to lose yourself in a role, and ministry is one of the easiest to get lost in.

For the reader who is unfamiliar with the ministry environment, let me share a few observations to help explain how esteem and expectations conspire to trap ministers in a role.

1. The community honors, esteems, and reveres its ministers. Therefore, it is easy to "get hooked" by this positive energy and become external-referenced on their approval.

2. There are virtually no boundaries in ministry. The community expects the minister to be "on call" day and night, ready and willing to help them deal with almost any kind of problem (not just spiritual ones).

    a. A minister does not have the internal permission other professionals have to be "off duty" or "taking time for self."

    b. The telephone rings frequently, day and night. Living in a rectory or parsonage allows for no privacy.

    c. Even when ministers do refer people to another source of help, it takes time to hear them out and point them in the right direction.

d. It is almost impossible to plan a day's work, for interruptions of all kinds (often legitimate) are likely. After all, ministers cannot predict when people will die and the family will need their services.

3. If the minister cannot (or does not) meet the community's expectations (with a smile, at that), he or she risks losing the esteem of the community — not to mention its financial support.

If you think this sounds like an impossible role to fill, you are correct. There is, however, a particular group of people in our culture who are superbly adapted for such an environment. I am talking about adult children of troubled families. The ministry environment is intense, unpredictable, and frequently crisis-oriented, all of which sounds normal to ACOA's. They grew up in such an environment and developed their survival roles in this dysfunctional milieu. Family Heroes and Caretakers in particular know how to gain approval and esteem by doing for others. It is hardly surprising that so many move into helping professions later in life.

What we see, then, is that the role of minister fits ACOA Heroes and Caretakers like a hand in a glove. The ministry work environment itself serves to support and perpetuate addictions; these codependents progress in their diseases. The role of minister becomes a trap, but giving up the role seems to require forfeiting the respect of the community.

I believe that burnout in ministry often happens because ACOA's have played out their role and have entered into chronic codependency. A role can keep one energized only for so long; after a while it destroys the spirit. Many of these burnouts (especially ordained and religious ministers) continue as ministers in the same way chronic alcoholics continue to drink. They no longer find joy in their ministry, but neither do they find joy in anything else. They merely hang on to the role as a drunk clings to the bottle.

Sadly, their leaders often allow the problem to continue year after year in the name of "respecting where people are in their pain" (a euphemism for the enabling picture of tolerating).

Of course, not all ministers are ACOA's; I, for example, am not an ACOA. What amazes me now, however, is how the ministerial environment enabled me to develop many codependent patterns. The esteem of the community (as well as the joy of helping others and expressing my gifts, no doubt) hooked me; the chaotic work environment fragmented my psyche, distorting my internal resources; the expectation to be all things to all people had me feeling constantly "on call"; rubbing shoulders with other addicted ministers set me up to be an enabler; and, to boot, I was ignorant of the dynamics of addiction and codependency. Because of my experience, I incline to the view that many who are not codependent when they enter the ministry will become so because of the ministerial environment.

Addictive Dynamics in the Institution

On a segment of *The MacNeil/Lehrer NewsHour,* several experts were discussing the problem of cocaine abuse in the United States. As might be expected, they all called for strict measures of law enforcement, prevention efforts, and treatment for individuals already addicted. Then, like a breath of fresh air, one of the panel members (a congressman) said: "We've been doing *all* these things for years and the problem only continues to *worsen!* What I'd like to know is *why* there is such an appetite for these chemicals in our country in the first place. What does this say about us as a society?"

Anne Wilson Schaef answered his question in her provocative book *When Society Becomes an Addict.* Schaef pointed out that society is not just a collection of individuals but a system with a life of its own. The life of this system is determined by the kinds of processes the system utilizes to perpetuate itself. She then goes on to identify processes that lead to the perpetuation of an addictive system, providing many examples of how extensively these processes operate in our culture today. Society itself can be viewed as a giant dysfunctional family; the appetite for chemicals and other addictive substances and processes comes from the addictive mind-set perpetuated in this family.

As I read Schaef's book it occurred to me that many of the addictive processes she identified were operative in the institutional Church (including here all Christian denominations). This insight was, for me, a missing piece in the puzzle of understanding addictions. The ACOA-addictive work environment connection was clear; deciding which came first was like the proverbial chicken-or-the-egg problem. What we must now begin to study is how the dynamics of dysfunctional families are replicated in the Church.

The insinuation that the institutional Church is anything but perfect will surely offend many. Any time we have a human organization perduring through the centuries, however, something of the dark side of our humanity is sure to creep in. A healthy organization — like a healthy person — is willing to allow this dark side to be brought into the light so it can be transformed. Unhealthy organizations — like addicts — defend their dysfunctional activities with lies, half-truths, counterattacks, or silence.

In reflecting on dysfunctional dynamics in the Church, we must recognize from the first that the Church — like a family — is not totally dysfunctional. It has both healthy and unhealthy dynamics operating within it. Imperfect though it may be, the Church is still God's instrument of salvation on this planet and continues in many ways to demonstrate fidelity to the gospel message with which it has been entrusted. Dysfunctional dynamics in the Church are tragic because they reduce its effectiveness in witnessing to the gospel and provide scandal to those weak in faith.

In his best-selling book on codependency, *Lost in the Shuffle,* Robert Subby proposes a helpful model for examining addictive dynamics in the institutional Church. According to Subby, what makes a system like a family or Church community healthy or unhealthy is the rules that govern the life of the system. In addictive systems, he writes, "These rules all serve to protect and isolate us from other people. They prevent us from sharing and exploring our real thoughts and feelings and they keep us from getting close to others." In short, they generate emotional pain, the fountainhead of codependency and all other addictions.

Subby lists nine rules that operate to some degree in all dysfunctional systems. To the extent that a system functions according to these rules, it will be dysfunctional. Those who get caught up in a dysfunctional system will also become unhealthy, for their growth will be both limited and distorted as a result of living by the rules of the system. The nine rules discussed by Subby are

1. It's not okay to talk about problems.
2. It's not okay to talk about or express feelings openly.
3. Communication is best if indirect, with something or someone between two other people. This is called triangulation.
4. Always be strong; always be good; always be perfect; always be happy. These expectations are unrealistic.
5. Don't be selfish (meaning here, self-loving).
6. Do as I say, not as I do.
7. It's not okay to be playful.
8. Don't rock the boat.
9. Don't talk about sex.

When I give workshops on codependency and ministry, I invite people to identify ways in which the institutional Church manifests these rules in its operations. Participants have been able to provide lists of examples for each rule at the various levels of governance: parish, diocese, and religious community; nationally and internationally.

It has become clear to me, too, that "pockets" of dysfunction exist in the Church — either geographic regions or levels of governance that are more dysfunctional than others. When, for example, the leader of a certain area or level was an addict or unhealthy in some manner, there was a greater preponderance of dysfunctional rules. This can be expected, for addicts re-create these dysfunctional dynamics wherever they go, and getting caught up in them leads to codependency.

What needs to be explored now is how these addictive dynamics have become part of the life of the institution. Here are a few questions that can serve to focus this discussion:

1. To what extent does the governance of the institution discourage or encourage open sharing, collegiality in decision-making, and intervention on problem areas?
2. To what extent does the institution discourage or encourage "boat-rocking," playfulness, and self-loving behavior?
3. To what extent does a hierarchical structure advocating political democracy model "Do as I say not as I do"?
4. Is it possible that dysfunctional dynamics in the institution attract dysfunctional leaders who perpetuate these dynamics?

Not only in my practice as a family substance-abuse counselor but also from personal experiences in family, working communities, and the Church, I repeatedly recognized that those who live in a sick system will themselves become sick in some way. The insights of systems theorists are valid; and their implications for the Church are many if we are willing to enter the painful process of self-reflection.

Just as individuals can change, however, so too can systems. I have seen some very sick family systems become healthy places for people to live and grow. Other systems at work and in the Church can change too.

The process of change for systems is the same as for individuals: recognition, re-centering, resolution, and retraining. The hardest part is recognition, for it is in this area that the emotional defenses block our way to honesty. Dualistic thinking, which holds that those who offer constructive criticism of the institution do not love the institution and should leave it, is one example of this defensiveness. Indeed, it is precisely because we love the institutional Church that we should offer constructive criticism at times.

Another obstacle to recognition sometimes comes from institutional leaders. In sick systems, some people receive greater payoffs than others from the system. In an alcoholic family, the alcoholic receives the payoffs of enabling; in a sick organization, a few leaders usually enjoy great power, control, and comfort because of the system. These leaders usually happen to be the ones responsible for the governance of the institution and, consequently, for the rules that direct the life of the system. To address the dysfunctional dynamics in the system is to threaten these leaders' power and control. At this point alcoholics sometimes threaten to cut family members off financially or harm them physically. Institutional leaders may threaten to use their power and authority in a similar punitive manner. In many institutions and societies, prophets are persecuted in one age and revered in the next.

The Church will be open to our prophets for change. Discernment is called for, to be sure. Change for the sake of change — or superficial change, with one sick system replacing another — is worthless. I believe, however, that the addiction-and-recovery model has much to offer in helping us discern the manner and direction of changes needed in the Church. We must get our own house in order if we are to be a more effective instrument of God in the world. That's what recovery is all about.

Addictive Behaviors Checklist

For each of the characteristics listed below, check the behaviors which apply to you.

	ALCOHOL/DRUG INTAKE	OVEREATING/UNDEREATING	APPROVAL-SEEKING	CARETAKING OTHERS	SEXUAL EXPRESSION	WORKING	GAMBLING	RELIGIOUS ACTIVITIES	WATCHING TELEVISION	SHOPPING
1. When I am feeling down, I frequently turn to this activity to feel better.										
2. I am uncomfortable with the way I indulge myself in this behavior.										
3. I sometimes lie about my involvement in this behavior.										
4. When I go without this activity for a while, I feel uncomfortable and panicky.										
5. My behavior in this area causes problems for me (physical, relational, and so on).										
6. My behavior in this area causes problems for others.										

7. I have tried to stop this behavior, but I inevitably go back to it.

8. When others confront me about this behavior, I become defensive.

9. Because of this behavior, I have cut back on healthy involvements.

10. If I could better control myself in this area, my life would be more manageable.

TOTALS

If you have one check in any area, it could indicate an addictive involvement. The more checks for any behavior, the more intense the addictive involvement.

APPENDIX TWO
Caretaking Versus Caring For

1. When I **caretake,** I assume responsibility for meeting the needs of others — even those needs which they should meet without me.
   When I **care for,** I do not do for others what they can and should do for themselves. I do for others what they truly need me to do.
2. When I **caretake,** I feel responsible for the feelings of others. If they are happy, I take credit; if they are sad, it is my fault.
   When I **care for,** I recognize that my behavior affects others. However, I know that it is their reaction to my behavior that produces their feelings. Therefore, I do not assume responsibility for the emotional states of others.
3. When I **caretake,** I expect others to live up to my expectations "for their own good." If they do not do it my way, I get upset.
   When I **care for,** I make no demands of others. If their behavior goes against my advice, I do not become upset.
4. When I **caretake,** I often try to control and manipulate others into doing things "my way." If it turns out right, I can take the credit; but if it turns out wrong, I feel guilty or else blame others.
   When I **care for,** I do not control. I give others the freedom to make their own mistakes and experience no guilt or blame when they do.
5. When I **caretake,** I focus so much on the needs of others that I neglect my own needs — maybe even lose a healthy sense of what my needs are.

When I **care for,** I remain alert to my needs and consider meeting my own needs as important as meeting the needs of others.

6. When I **caretake,** I see others as an extension of myself. Therefore, I do not really see them for themselves; I see them *for* myself. I have lost my boundaries in the relationship.

   When I **care for,** I retain a sense of my own boundaries. I can see other people for who they are in themselves.

7. When I **caretake,** I often feel tired, burdened, and resentful because so much of my personal energy is tied up in the welfare of others.

   When I **care for,** I feel relaxed, free, and peaceful because I have more energy within myself.

8. When I **caretake,** I do not love others.

   When I **care for,** I truly love others.

APPENDIX THREE
The Twelve Steps
of Alcoholics Anonymous

1. We admitted we were powerless over alcohol — that our lives had become unmanageable.
2. Came to believe that a Power greater than ourselves could restore us to sanity.
3. Made a decision to turn our will and our lives over to the care of God as we understood Him.
4. Made a searching and fearless moral inventory of ourselves.
5. Admitted to God, to ourselves, and to another human being the exact nature of our wrongs.
6. Were entirely ready to have God remove all these defects of character.
7. Humbly asked Him to remove our shortcomings.
8. Made a list of all persons we had harmed, and became willing to make amends to them all.
9. Made direct amends to such people wherever possible, except when to do so would injure them or others.
10. Continued to take personal inventory and when we were wrong promptly admitted it.
11. Sought through prayer and meditation to improve our conscious contact with God as we understood Him praying only for knowledge of His will for us and the power to carry that out.
12. Having had a spiritual awakening as a result of these steps, we tried to carry this message to alcoholics, and to practice these principles in all our affairs.

Note: These Twelve Steps can be used as a program of recovery from any addiction. Simply replace the word "alcohol" with the addictive behavior (example: caretaking, sexual expression, shopping) and then do the work each step requires.

For guidance on using the Twelve Steps as a process for overcoming selfishness in a Christian spiritual context, see my book *Becoming a New Person: Twelve Steps to Christian Growth,* Liguori Publications, One Liguori Drive, Liguori, MO 63057-9999.

Suggested Reading

Beattie, Melody. *Codependent No More: How to Stop Controlling Others and Start Caring for Yourself.* San Francisco: Harper & Row, 1988.

Berry, Carmen Renee. *When Helping You Is Hurting Me: Escaping the Messiah Trap.* New York: Harper & Row, 1988.

Black, Claudia. *Repeat After Me.* Denver: MAC Printing and Publications, 1985.

Johnson, Vernon E. *I'll Quit Tomorrow.* San Francisco: Harper & Row, 1980.

McAuliffe, Robert M., Ph.D., and Mary Boesen, Ph.D. *The Essentials of Chemical Dependency.* Minneapolis: The American Chemical Dependency Society, 1975.

St. Romain, Philip. *Becoming a New Person: Twelve Steps to Christian Growth.* Liguori, MO: Liguori Publications, 1984.

_____. *Building Character in Young People.* Gretna: Pelican Publishing Co., 1986.

_____. *Pathways to Serenity.* Liguori, MO: Liguori, Publications, 1988.

_____. *Lessons in Loving: Developing Relationship Skills.* Liguori, MO: Liguori Publications, 1988.

Schaef, Anne Wilson and Diane Fassel. *The Addictive Organization.* San Francisco: Harper & Row, 1988.

Schaef, Anne Wilson. *Co-Dependence: Misunderstood-Mistreated.* San Francisco: Harper & Row, 1986.

_____. *When Society Becomes an Addict.* San Francisco: Harper & Row, 1987.

Subby, Robert. *Lost in the Shuffle: The Co-Dependent Reality.* Pompano Beach: Health Communications, 1987.

Woititz, Janet G. *Adult Children of Alcoholics.* Hollywood, FL: Health Communications, Inc., 1983.